Oral Commentaries

By

Drikung Kagyü Teachers

In

San Francisco

Oral Commentaries

By

His Holiness Drikung Kyabgön Chetsang Rinpoche

On the Refuge Vow Ceremony Amitabha Buddha and the Pureland of Dewachen and Vajrakilaya

Translated by Michael Lewis
Transcribed by
Könchog Gönpo Gyaltsen (Jeffery Beach)

Refuge Vow Ceremony

Today I am giving refuge. We are engaged in the ceremony of taking refuge. We say that we take refuge, or go for refuge to the Buddha, the Dharma, and the Sangha. Those are the Three Objects of Refuge. Let us examine what these Three Objects of Refuge mean. First of all, in English and in Sanskrit, the name 'Buddha' seems to indicate or point to a particular person, but in actuality the meaning of 'Buddha' is a state of awakening, which is composed of two factors. In Tibetan, the word is 'Sangye'. The first syllable of the word is 'Sang', Sang means to have completely purified the mindstream of all the stains and defilements deriving from ignorance, or unknowing, in other words the primitive beliefs about the nature of reality. It is the elimination all faults, or negativity, from the mindstream. The second syllable is 'gye', which means to completely awaken and maximize all positive qualities innate to the mind itself. So it is said that essentially our own minds are awakened, they have awakened qualities. Bringing those awakened qualities to the fore is what is meant by 'gye'. Then, putting the two syllables together is what is meant by the term 'Buddha' in the Tibetan teachings. This is something we have in us and can cultivate, because it is the seed of what we are. Now, there are three objects of refuge or three sources of refuge: Buddha, Dharma, and Sangha. Those three are one, but they are not one single manifestation, they are three manifestations. The Buddha can be said to be the guide, or the one who

9

shows the path, he is compared to the pilot of a boat. It is said that we need to traverse the infinite ocean of suffering of cyclic existence and reach the other shore, which is freedom from this suffering. In order to that, we need a pilot, or teacher, someone who knows the way. The teacher is the Buddha. The one who demonstrates the perfect path that leads to the complete cleansing and purification of the mindstream of all its stains and defilements, bringing to the fore and maximizing all positive qualities. The Dharma is the path the Buddha demonstrates which actually leads to liberation from cyclic existence. Those who help us along the way, guiding us, and 'fine tuning' our path, are the Sangha. These are the three manifestations, the three jewels of refuge. When taking refuge according to the procedure of the Great Vehicle (Mahayana), one should understand that one is seeking refuge for protection not for oneself alone, and not for any self-interest. Rather one cultivates the mindset that one is going for refuge in order to liberate all sentient beings.

As for the enactment of the taking of refuge, one begins the process by making obeisance (prostrating) in a physical way. The start of prostrations begins by the folding of the hands in a particular way. The hands should be held together, with the thumbs tucked together in an elegant way. This is actually symbolic of a lotus blossom, which one offers to the objects of refuge to receive the benevolence of the sources of refuge. There are many ways this can be explained. In general, you fold the hands in prayer gesture, tuck the thumbs together, and begin making prostrations, touching the hands to three places. Those three points, the forehead, throat, and heart chakras, symbolize that you go for refuge with your body, speech, and mind. The next act, the actual prostrating, symbolizes and subsumes the performance of refuge. You touch your two hands, two knees, and forehead to the ground. Therefore, there are five points symbolizing the yearning to overcome the five primary poison mindsets of ignorance, attachment, aversion, jealousy, and arrogance. Touching these five points of the body to the ground means that you are going for refuge to overcome the virulent effects of those five poisons.

(At this point, the actual ceremony of taking refuge was performed, after which His Holiness resumed His teaching.)

Now, you should all understand that you have just undergone an important experience. You have actually taken refuge. You have gone for refuge. This means that from this day forward you should develop a powerful impetus to practice Buddhadharma, to practice the teachings of the Buddha. At least every day, you should make three prostrations and you can pray the short prayer of refuge. If you want to practice more extensively on a daily basis, you can practice preliminary refuge practices that are available in text form. This is a very great occasion. You have invited into your lives something very important and powerful. You should rejoice in that fact. Another reason that the taking of refuge is so special and so important is that it actually constitutes a level of ordination into the practice of Buddhism. There are various levels of what can be called ordination. You can be an ordained layperson where you can take vows to avoid the Ten Non-Virtues and practice the Ten Virtues of body speech and mind. You can be a novice monk or nun. You can be a fully ordained monk or nun. You can be a tantrika. There are many levels of ordination and ordained practice in the world. Taking refuge is the gateway into all of them. In addition, in the secret mantra Vajrayana, the main thing is empowerment and there is no way to attain empowerment without refuge. Therefore, it can be said that refuge is the foundation and the laying of the foundation is extremely important. Therefore, this is an extremely important occasion in which you participated this morning.

It is said that the fundamental characteristics of the teachings of the Buddha and the practices of Buddhism are the interrelation of all things. The understanding of this interrelationship exists within the essence of Buddhism. Therefore, it is said that the Compassion of the Buddhas is related to the need of living beings. The compassion of the Buddhas is like a hook. When sentient beings take refuge as you have today, it is as if you have put a ring that the hook can catch. Therefore, the hook and the ring are interrelated. The taking of refuge is the establishment of the ring in your being that can be hooked by the Compassion of the Buddhas. This is the entrance into all practice. If you wish to practice, you may practice. In any case, by undergoing this particular ceremony you received the blessing of the enlightened being we call Buddha. You have received the transference into your own mindstreams of the positive energy of the enlightened being we call Buddha. As far as the teachings of the Buddha are concerned, they are innumerable. It is said that there are 84,000 categories of the teachings and practices within the totality of Buddhadharma. The essence of

12

them all, if one wishes to apply them to oneself is to overcome ignorance, sins, stains, defilements, and negativities of emotions and primitive beliefs about the nature of reality through practice. If we were to boil it all down into a single phrase it would be this: "Do not enact any non-virtue, even the smallest non-virtue avoid, do everything positive; tame and train your own mind". This is the essence of the teachings of the Buddha. Another way to look at taking refuge is that you enter into a partnership with the Buddha. We can say that there is a necessary relationship involved. It is said that the Buddha, by Himself, cannot liberate sentient beings from the effects of their negative karma. For example, the Buddha cannot wash away your obscurations with His hand. There needs to be a relationship between the way shown, the techniques given by the Buddha, and your own practice. It is like doing work on a computer: there needs to be both hardware and software for the work to be done. It is not something that can be done with the click of a computer key. It is not something that manifests automatically, but rather it is something you have to take an active part. Your own liberation will result from the powerful teachings of the Enlightened Being given to you as well as your own application of effort to these teachings. You need to practice in order to accumulate merit and eliminate the negativity of past karma, thereby opening the way to your own realization of the actual nature of being itself, which is the essence of Dharma. The Buddha has shown the way, now it is up to you to tread that path. As for the teachings of the Buddha, the Speech of the Buddha, you first need to hear the teachings, to take the teachings, to hear the Words of the Buddha. Then you need to think about

13

what you heard, contemplate what you have heard. Investigate what you have heard. Test it, try it out, and see if it works. Then you need to meditate on what you have contemplated. The Buddha never recommended the dependence on instantaneous blind faith. Rather, he recommended investigation, testing, weighing, comparing, and contrasting: really getting into it. Then, because of what you discovered, based on discovering the qualities of the teachings in your lives. Developing faith should be something that is as valued as gold: you test it, scratch it put it in various chemicals, it passed all the tests, and you say: "AH this is really gold!" Then you value it appropriately. The Buddhadharma is like that, all the teachings and practices within Buddhism are like that. You hear them, you think about them, you try them out, and you see how they work for you. When they work for you, you develop faith, a faith that is a reasoned faith. It is not a meaningless leap of faith; rather it is based upon practical direct experience. The Buddha actually said "I don't want people developing faith out of respect for me, or because they got a big flash from me. Practice what I teach, and if it works for you, then develop faith in me." Don't do it just out of respect for the outer trappings, but actually experience the inner essence of the teachings for yourself. That is the solid rationale of faith that the Buddha always recommended.

It is important to understand that you have done something here by going for refuge that has many benefits. These many positive effects will begin to be felt by you in your lives and your mindstreams. In general, it can be said that you have entered the path to liberation. On a relative plane, it said that you have averted much harm that might otherwise have come to you. You will not be harmed or hurt in any way by the negative machinations of humans or non-human obstructers. The many sins, stains, and defilements that you have accumulated from beginningless time until now in your mindstreams have been cleansed and purified through the act of taking refuge alone. Vast stores of merit have been planted in your mindstreams. You have assured yourselves of something that can be of benefit to you, even at the moment of death. These are some of the relative benefits you acquired by taking refuge this morning.

Amitabha Buddha and the Pureland of Dewachen

This morning His Holiness is going to give teachings concerning Amitabha Buddha, the Buddha of Boundless Light, and His Pureland. In conjunction with the teachings in general, this afternoon, His Holiness will teach how to obtain the transference of consciousness to the Pureland of Amitabha Buddha through this practice. Specifically, He will teach you how to practice the text of which all of you should get a copy. It is the daily sadhana for the practice of Amitabha Buddha. Yesterday, you received that empowerment.

Generally, it can be said that there are many Purelands, many paradises of Enlightened Beings we call Buddhas. The Pureland of Great Bliss of the Buddha of Boundless Light, Amitabha, is quite a unique place. There are Purelands in the four directions, East, South, West, North, and in the center. Among them, the Pureland of Amitabha is the easiest to get to and therefore quite special. By formulating a special aspiration to be reborn in the Pureland of Great Bliss, one can accomplish the transference of one's consciousness to that Pureland. The power of prayer, the power of devoted and fervent aspiration, is all that is necessary. It is said that the Pureland of Amitabha Buddha, in relation to our universe, is in the western direction and above our universe. We have to adopt a cosmic view and realize that there are many world systems throughout space. This is a very vast system of which I am speaking. Let us get our bearings here. What I am speaking of, in terms of the grand scheme of things, works like this: Lord Buddha Shakyamuni is the chief enlightened being in one great chiliocosm. This means that our entire known universe, with its suns and moons and stars and planets, is one unit. Multiply that by one thousand and then multiply that by one thousand and multiply that by one thousand. That is one trichiliocosm. Lord Buddha Shakyamuni is the lord of one of those. The realm of the Buddha of Boundless Light goes beyond even that cosmic scale. I am teaching right now, from a prayer for expressing this powerful aspiration to be reborn in the Pureland of Great Bliss, composed by Karma Chagne Rinpoche. In the prayer, Karma Chagne Rinpoche says the Pureland of Great Bliss is on such a vast scale, so greatly distant from our ordinary reality, our flesh eyes can never behold it. It is not something that can be beheld physically. It is so vast; its scale is incommensurate with any kind of scale we know that it is beyond the possibility for our senses to perceive. It is so far and vast, so completely beyond our abilities to measure. We can see stars and travel to the moon, but we will never be able to appropriate to the reaching range our senses the actuality of Land of Great Bliss. It is that vast and distant from our ordinary thinking and perceiving. In that sense, it cannot be reached by any material means. However, our own minds, when purified, when stripped of their faults, when returned to their own primordially pristine condition can directly experience the reality of the Pureland of Great Bliss. The way to perceive the Pureland is through the mind, not through the senses. So, establish that vision in your mind and imagine that, in the center of the vast, all-encompassing

Land of Great Bliss, resides the Lord of the Pureland: the Buddha Amitabha, the Buddha of Boundless Light. He is red in color and he looks like Shakyamuni Buddha. He has all the 80 major marks and the 32 minor signs of a fully enlightened manifestation of Nirmanakaya. He has, for example, the crown protuberance that you see on the statues and thangkas of Lord Buddha. He has wheels on His hands and so forth, so, as you can see there are many different signs. He holds His hands in the posture on meditative equipoise, the Dhyana Mudra, and in His hands is a begging bowl. He looks quite like Shakyamuni Buddha. However, His skin is a deep, ruby red color. He is resplendent and radiant. He sits on top of a lotus and moon seat. Behind His back is the Wish Fulfilling Tree. To His right is Lord Avalokiteshvara, Chenrezig, white in body color. To His left is Vajrapani, the Lord of Powerful Means. These are the three chief lords of the Pureland of Great Bliss. To give a little bit of history of the formation of the Pureland of Great Bliss of Buddha Amitabha, it is a Pureland, which has no flaws. It is perfect in every way. The realization of that Pureland did come without cause. What was this cause of this perfect paradise? Very many aeons ago, before he was a Buddha, the Buddha Amitabha was a monk whose name was Dharmakara, which literally translated means 'the origin of Dharma'. When He was in training as a bodhisattva, He formulated a series of prayers, or powerful aspirations, about the way things should be when He becomes completely enlightened. He said, "There are so many Purelands that exist and can be reached by those sentient beings who abandoned non-virtue, who accumulated a great deal of merit, and assiduously practiced the Dharma. They can reach those Purelands, but that is very difficult. What about all those who have not abandoned non-virtue, who have not accumulated a great deal of merit, and cannot practice in a rigorous way? Let me establish a Pureland that can be easily reached by them. May I liberate all those sentient beings who don't have those supernal qualities of the practitioners that reach the other Purelands of all the other Buddhas". There are many versions of the prayer (or vows), of Amitabha Buddha formulated when He was Dharmakara. There are 500 different versions of the prayer in Tibet alone. In China there are many texts concerning the formulation of the Great Vows of Amitabha. In general, it can be said that all of His powerful aspirations can be subsumed under 48 Great Vows. The Pureland of Great Bliss was brought into reality because of one of the 48 Great Vows. This is the cause for the existence of Pureland of great Bliss. This Pureland does not exist causelessly, nothing does. The cause for it was the activity of the bodhisattva who became the Buddha Amitabha. In general, all the Buddhas hold all sentient beings in the core of their heart with love and compassion. Out of their great compassion, they formulate powerful aspirations. They make great vows. They work through many lifetimes, while in training as bodhisattvas before they became Buddhas to affect all sentient beings in vast variety of ways. Just as you can create fire by rubbing two sticks together, long enough and hard enough, so, by the accumulation of merit and primordial wisdom, anything can be accomplished. What was accomplished, in this case, was the establishment of the Pureland of Great Bliss in the western direction of our universe by the Buddha Amitabha through His vast store of merit and primordial wisdom. Let us, again, examine the metaphor of the two sticks that are needed to create fire. Fire does not spring automatically from one stick. You need two sticks and you need the effort of rubbing them together in a particular way over a period of time. Eventually a spark leaps from the conjunction of the sticks and fire begins. In a similar way, all phenomena, all reality, all dharmas, manifest by the conjunction of emptiness and interdependent origination. Everything is totally interrelated with every other thing. That is called interdependent origination. That is one stick. The other stick is emptiness: the truth of emptiness, the complete lack of inherent existence of any phenomena. The two sticks together are the actual nature of reality. This is true of everything, of all realities. Leave aside the Pureland for a moment and let us examine the realm in which we live. Our world is the same. Our world is the product of non-dual union of clarity and emptiness, of appearance and emptiness. Things appear in a completely unimpeded way, and yet they have no essence. Their essence is empty. That means that all possibilities of experience derive from the non-dual union of appearance and emptiness. Let us examine the manifestation of our world or of the Pureland. Everything is not a mere emptiness because it appears, does it not? We can clearly see everything. Everything seems to have existence and everything seems to have a material basis in our world. That is the side of the equation indicating the clear manifestation of phenomena, of experiences[1]. However, that side

---

[1]Phenomena and experience are the same word in Tibetan: 'Nangwa.' Nangwa means phenomena,

could not be if it were not for emptiness. If anything, at all, had solid substantial, material, inherent existence, nothing could exist. It is because of emptiness that things can manifest as appearances. Only because there is emptiness, can anything exist at all. Without emptiness, there would only be one indissoluble monolithic blob. There would only be one thing, if that. Nothing could possibly come into relative existence without the ultimate grounding in emptiness. Therefore, it is because of emptiness that our world exists. Because of emptiness, the Pureland of Great Bliss was established through the power of the aspiration, the accumulation of merit, and the primordial wisdom of the enlightened being Amitabha. This is quite difficult to understand if you are new to Buddhism, I understand that, but it is only because there is emptiness that there is appearance. Lets us now continue with our examination of the particular qualities of the Pureland formulated by the aspiration of Amitabha Buddha know as the Land of Dewachen. There are many other buddhafields, as has been said, but in order to reach them, one must attain quite an exalted status. For example to reach the Pureland of another Buddha, it is necessary to be a tenth stage bodhisattva, or approaching the portals of complete and perfect enlightenment, and to have accumulated a great deal of merit. It is very difficult for ordinary sentient beings to aspire to this. For us, Amitabha Buddha formulated His great powerful prayers of aspiration. Although His Pureland seems to be quite far from our world, it is relatively easy to reach for sentient

---

appearance, and lighting up from within the ground of being. It has many meanings.

beings like us. This is due to the power of Amitabha Buddha's prayers and vows. As was said before, there exist many versions of the vows, prayers, and aspirations of Amitabha Buddha. To briefly encompass them in a single statement, it need be said that the essence of the vows, prayers, and aspirations are: "May a Pureland be established that is reachable by ordinary sentient beings of impure karma, beings of karmic evil, which have not abandoned non-virtue." When you reach the Purelands of other Buddhas, because of exalted status before going there, you become enlightened. In the case of Dewachen, you can get there, but it does not mean you become enlightened. What happens is that you will not revert to cyclic existence; rather, you will have, instead, all the positive and auspicious conditions for the accumulation of merit and primordial wisdom. You will be able to abandon all non-virtue there and practice to tame and train your mind until such point you are ripe for enlightenment. That is then a general introduction to the Land of Great Bliss.

Now I will give an explanation of prayer aspiring to be reborn in the Land of Dewachen composed by Karma Chagne Rag-Astrs Rinpoche. To begin with, I will start with a description of the topography of the Pureland itself. The earth is not like the earth on our world. It is not, rough, and covered with stones. It is completely smooth and completely even. It is composed of jewel dust. In the Pureland of Great Bliss, you always have a feeling of expansive view. It is very vast. There are no alterations of light and shade. A universal all-pervasive light derives from the physical form of the Buddha of Boundless Light, Amitabha. The entire realm is infused with the luminosity of the enlightened body of Buddha

Amitabha. The ground is not hard. It is soft and if you fall on it, you would bounce. You would not stub your toe. Everything is very soft in Dewachen. As for the flora of Dewachen, trees, which are abundant, are wish fulfilling jewel trees, trees that grant you whatever you need. The branches are filled with birds of various kinds. They are all emanations of Amitabha Buddha. They have beautiful melodious voices. Rather than ordinary bird song, they sing Dharma teachings in such a way as to delight and pacify the mind. Everyone there who hears the melodious sound of the Dharma become peaceful, happy, and content. There are many rivers and streams, brooks and rivulets. The water is not ordinary water. It is perfume. There are pools where you can rest and have a dip in perfumed waters. The land is filled with gloriously scented lotus blossoms, which open and emanate, from the pollen heart of each lotus, an abundance of light rays. On the tip of each light ray, is a Buddha. The Buddhas all teach the Dharma. They teach the Dharma in such a way that the mind is completely stripped of any negative emotions. In the Land of Dewachen, there is no sickness, no poverty, no old age, and no death. There is no distinction between one being and another. All are equally beautiful. All are equally replete with all positive qualities. There are no faults, no lacks, no stains, no suffering of any kind, not even the word 'suffering' can be heard in the Pureland of Great Bliss.

The way to take birth in Dewachen is to formulate a great faith and aspiration concerning the Pureland, and have a desire to be born there. When you give birth there, you are not born through any ordinary process. In our world, we all arrive in pain and travail in sorrow. Birth is a painful process here. In Dewachen, you are not born through a womb, but rather you are magically born in the pollen heart of a lotus blossom. If you pray with single-pointed concentration and great fervent faith to be born there, you will be born there. If you harbor any doubt, you will still be born there, but you will be born inside a closed lotus blossom. You are bathed in the effulgent light of the Buddha but you cannot see all the qualities of the Pureland and you cannot wander about at will. You are in the closed lotus blossom until the last vestiges of doubt and negativity are eliminated. Then the lotus blossom will open, if you have no doubt, whatsoever you are born in an open lotus. This pertains to the type of aspiration you make to be reborn in the Pureland that you make at the moment of death. Keep in mind this very important distinction between the two different births in the Pureland. It is very important to formulate the proper aspiration of rebirth at the moment of death. Do this powerfully without any doubt. If you allow doubt to enter your mind, you will be born in the closed lotus blossom. If you formulate this powerful aspiration at the moment of death then, without any intervening experience, take birth in the pollen heart of an open lotus blossom in the presence of the Buddha of Boundless Light, Amitabha. One of the marvelous qualities of being reborn in the Pureland of Great Bliss is this: if you had read the 'travel brochures' for other Purelands, you could go there immediately just wishing it. You can magically transport to any of the other Purelands by simply formulating the wish to go there. From this world, you cannot immediately go to any other Pureland, but from the Pureland of Great Bliss, you can. You have passport, visas, and all tickets necessary to go to any Pureland of any Buddha, in any direction any time you wish.

When you take birth in the open lotus blossom, you are not perfect yet. You have eliminated all negativities from your mindstream, but you take birth in a form that possesses many positive qualities that are like those of a Buddha though you are not yet a Buddha. You are born with a resplendent golden body. You have telepathic and extrasensory powers. There are five types of extrasensory powers you enjoy. Another quality you possess as a neonate is all the things that you need to offer to the Buddhas you now perceive with your physical eyes are automatically manifested from your hands. Thereby you can easily accumulate merit and perfect it to accumulate wisdom. Furthermore, the accumulation of merit and wisdom results, ultimately in Buddhahood takes place very quickly in the Pureland of Great Bliss. As opposed to other Purelands, the process of accumulating merit and wisdom is very rapid in Dewachen. Buddha Shakyamuni himself said: "Therefore to pray to be reborn in Dewachen accumulates as much merit as if you were to offer the seven types of jewels and other precious substances filling the three thousand fold world systems (mentioned earlier)." In general, we can say that any sentient being that hears the name of Amitabha Buddha (in accordance with Amitabha Buddha's Great Vows) formulates the aspiration to be reborn in Dewachen and engages in that practice can be reborn in Dewachen. It is more difficult for those who have accumulated the negativity of the five inexpiable sins[2].

---

[2] Known as the Five Great Crimes of Immediate Retribution, they are: killing your own father, killing

Still, even for such great sinners, if they practice strongly, it is possible for them even to attain rebirth in Dewachen. In brief, concerning the teachings of the Buddha Amitabha and the Pureland of Great Bliss, in all Mahayana countries this practice is very prevalent. Why is this so? It is because of the nature of the vows of Amitabha Buddha. The practice of Amitabha Buddha and the Pureland is geared to ordinary people. Anyone can engage in the practice. You do not have to be a great exalted being who has abandoned all non-virtue. You do not have to be a superb practitioner. Depending upon the power of the vows of Amitabha Buddha, you can engage in this practice. This is a Sutrayana practice. Therefore, it is something that can work for anyone. It is very democratic and it is available to all.

---

your own mother, killing your teacher (lama), killing an arhat, drawing blood from the body of the Buddha. These sins might seem quite removed from anything we might engage in, however, there are analogous sins that are committed more frequently and have the same effect. They are: killing a monk, killing a nun, killing a novice monk or nun, causing a nun to lose her vows (meaning to sexually abuse a nun), destroying (or damaging) a stupa or a statue of the Buddha.

Question and Answers

Question
"Are there opportunities, once you have obtained birth in the Pureland, to return to this world to help sentient beings attain enlightenment?"

Answer
"The purpose of attaining rebirth in the Pureland of Great Bliss is to attain Buddhahood. Therefore, the meaning of the Pureland of Great Bliss is that you have attained all the conditions that are auspicious and are militate towards the gaining of complete and perfect enlightenment. When you become completely enlightened, it is not one-sided enlightenment that rests in Nirvana. It is the Mahayana enlightenment which, grounded in emptiness, realizes that nirvana and samsara are something not to attach to. The keynote of all Mahayana practice is Great Compassion. The Pureland, itself, was established through the power of the Great Compassion of Amitabha Buddha. If you realize emptiness, then, compassion automatically manifests. That emptiness and compassion, together, which constitute Buddhahood, also constitute complete and perfect freedom. That is, finally, the meaning of freedom. When you become that free, you are not restricted to the Pureland of Great Bliss. You can to any Pureland you want. You can enact any other mode of manifestation you desire. You manifest ceaselessly in

an infinite variety of ways for the welfare of all living beings."

Question
"On the one hand it sounds very simple to achieve rebirth in Dewachen. On the other hand, in order to have that true bliss at that moment one would have to have to establish oneself, truly wishing to achieve bodhicitta in one's being. So that it seems to be the great challenge of being here is to establish the wish to help other beings and not just oneself. So perhaps it is not so easy."

Answer
"The taking of rebirth in Dewachen is only difficult if you committed one of the Five Inexpiable Sins of Great Retribution. If you have not committed one of them, then is quite easy, because all you need to do is to depend upon the power of the forming of powerful aspirations to have rebirth in Dewachen. What that does is to unite you with the antidote to all your other obscurations and non-virtue. That is the power of the vow of Amitabha Buddha. The other element kicks in when you formulate the aspiration to connect with this practice and to be reborn the Pureland. Another reason why it is quite easy to attain rebirth is that the moment of death is every moment. The Dharma teaches that all things are in a state of flux. All things are impermanent and tending towards death all the time, therefore in every moment, something dies and something takes rebirth. How your mind is directed is how your experience will be. Your present thought will lead to your subsequent experience. If you establish a continuity of aspiration from moment to moment,

understanding that any moment could be the moment of death, at every moment you yearn to be reborn in Dewachen, you establish that continuity of aspiration. That will be your experience. The cause in that moment will create the effect in the next moment. Everything is mental transformation (His Holiness speaking in English)."

Question
"Rinpoche, can you tell us more about the light in closed lotus? How does that light them?"

Answer
"The light bathes all and everything in the Land of Great Bliss. Like everything else, in and about the Land of Great Bliss, it is an emanation of Amitabha Buddha. It is all part of Amitabha Buddha. Everything that is perceivable in Dewachen is an extension of Amitabha Buddha. The light is the Light of Compassion. It is Light of Compassion that ripens sentient beings."

Question
Unintelligible[3]

Answer
"The formulation of the prayer to take rebirth in Dewachen is an individual matter. You cannot develop an aspiration on someone else's behalf. However, you can help someone else by repeating to them the name of Amitabha and acquainting them with the existence

---

[3] The question seems to ask whether one can say the aspiration prayer to take rebirth in Dewachen for other sentient beings.

of Amitabha in the Pureland. It is said that even hearing the name Amitabha is very beneficial. Another thing you can do to help others is at the moment of another's death that you can do Amitabha practice of various kinds. For example, at the moment of death, you can do Ph'owa, and that is a practice of transferring that person's consciousness from their dying body. Other rituals and pujas are done at that time. There is one called Shitje. It is ritual done at the moment of death. Many things can be done even if the person has already died. Their consciousness principle is addressed and instructed in various ways."

Question
Unintelligible question from the audience

Answer
"We have to talk a little about emptiness. The teachings of emptiness in no way claim that what we perceive does not exist absolutely. We are not saying that things made of atoms and molecules and have material reality literally do not exist, and in that sense, illusory. We are saying that they have no self-nature. They have no inherent existence. They have no solid, substantial, reality that corresponds to their mode of appearance. They seem to be inherently existent, yet they are not. This is the teaching of the great Middle Way School, Madhyamika. There a couple of different schools of thought here, the Mind-Only School (Cittimatra) says that everything is mind. The only thing that truly exists is the mind itself and everything else is a projection of the mind. Mahamudra teachings say that the actual nature of reality is such that it transcends postulation of either existence or non-existence, or both, or neither.

31

This is called the 'Four Extremes'. The Mahamudra view transcends them. From our relative level of truth in Tibetan, they say 'Kun-Zop Dempa' which is a fascinating phrase[4]. 'Dempa' means truth. 'Kun-Zop' means completely false. Therefore, the 'completely false truth', the relative truth is a result of our mistaken perception. We perceive things to have inherent existence when they really do not. Our minds grasp at what we perceive as solid and real. Because of that mental grasping, we reify that which is in fact empty. That is a mistake. That is an error. All appearances are our experience. They are experienced by and in our own minds. Other than that, there is no possibility of experience. All external appearance is a mental projection in the sense that it is experienced by the mind. It has no solid inherent existence from its own side. That is a mistake in perception."

Question.
"Is there any way in which one can be in the Pureland, aside from literally at the end of existence? On the other hand, is this something that can be reached in this present existence? Can the Pureland be accessed in this life?"

Answer
"Yes, when the last breath has been exhaled, before the next breath is inhaled. At that moment, there is a death and a rebirth. You can experience the Pureland there in the interval between breaths."

---

[4] Translator's comment.

Question.

"Rinpoche, you say that you can experience the Pureland in that interval, in that case, what is the Pureland?"

Answer

"What is the Pureland really? The Pureland is one's own stainless primordial awareness. If, from moment to moment, you regain and retain your own primordial enlightened nature: that is the Pureland. Everything comes from your own mind. Understand that, remain there: that is the Pureland."

Question.

"If interdependent origination arises in emptiness. Then, how can this be if there is no elaboration in emptiness?"

Answer.

"Emptiness and interdependent origination are non-dual. They are one. Even to say non-dual is to miss the mark, because that implies that there might have been a duality that was overcome. From the beginningless beginning, they have always been one. There is no difference between them. It is not like there are two divisions. When you see emptiness and interdependent origination dualistically, it is the extrapolation of samsara, cyclic existence. Overcome duality and you see cause and effect at the same time. Then everything arises together. That is complete, non-dual emptiness and interdependent origination. In the text, many examples are used to illustrate this truth of the non-dual union of emptiness and interdependent origination. Nevertheless, let us take, for example, this cup. As a relative manifestation or appearance that be experienced by our perceptual mechanisms, the cup is something that is composite. It is made of smaller particles. Is it not? It is made of atoms and molecules that become particular substances: earth, air, fire, and water. All of those things are combined in such a way as to produce what we call a cup. Then it is decorated, painted, and carved. That is something that is made in Tibetan we say 'Dütshe': composite, something that has been created. Causes and conditions have been brought together in such a way to create a relatively existent manifestation that we can use and interact with and perceive as what we call a cup. However, from its own side, independent of causes and conditions, there is no 'cupness'. There is nothing arising as the 'cup' in and of itself apart from that entire process of causes and conditions coming together. It has no essence. Its essence is empty. In the 'Prajña Paramita Hydraya' Sutra, the 'Heart Sutra', it says, "Form is emptiness, and emptiness is form. Other than emptiness there is no form, other than form there is no emptiness." All phenomena have that exact same nature. Whatever is experienced within either cyclic existence, or its transcendence, has that exact same nature. Its essence is empty and it is experienced as a result of interdependent origination. To perceive things as alternate visions of emptiness and interdependent origination is to remain an ordinary sentient being. To overcome the dualistic vision, to perceive things simultaneously as emptiness and interdependent origination, is to be Buddha. The great Arya Nagarjuna said: "Cyclic existence and its transcendence (samsara and nirvana) are not two. Understanding the nature of cyclic existence in itself is transcendence."

On the Short Sadhana of Amitabha Buddha and the Pureland of Dewachen

We begin on page 2 of the text. The first word is 'Namo'. ' Namo' means, "I bow down to, prostrate to, or make obeisance to". To whom? To the Three Jewels, the Buddha, the Dharma, and the Sangha. In addition to, or as another mode of manifestation of the Three Jewels, there is what is called 'The Three Roots'. They are one's teachers, the lamas; the chosen deities, the Yidams; and the Dakinis who are the forces of inspiration manifesting as enlightened females. All beings who have attained any stature of enlightenment: Buddhas, Bodhisattvas, any of those in whose mind has arisen enlightenment. In all of them, I go for refuge for the sake of establishing all sentient beings in the state of Buddhahood. In this one stanza of four lines, there are two processes, where both refuge and the generation of bodhicitta are contained. The first two lines constitute the refuge. Then the purpose for going for refuge is to place all sentient beings in the state of enlightenment; I will generate the mind of enlightenment. In this one sloka[5], two things are accomplished: going for refuge and the establishment of bodhicitta. These are the preliminary steps for entering the practice of the sadhana. Three things have been accomplished already. One has been obeisance. The second is the taking of refuge. The third is the generation of bodhicitta. One repeats this stanza three times.

---

[5] Stanza

Now one can engage in the main body of the practice. However, to engage in the practice, first, let go of your perception of yourself as an ordinary flesh and blood person, and your environment as being ordinary. Dissolve everything into emptiness. Then, from emptiness itself, arises the remainder of the practice. The dissolution of all ordinary perception into emptiness and rising of all subsequent practice from emptiness is implicit in the first syllable of this line: the syllable 'AH'. It is said that the syllable AH is the supreme sound. It is the seed of all other letters, syllables, and sounds. AH is the thirtieth letter of the Tibetan alphabet, making it the culmination of the meaning, the sound, the intention, and the vibrational frequencies of all the other letters. It is the implicit underlying, deep meaning of, and the culmination of all the other letters and all the other sounds. In the text of the "Manjushri Namsanghati", it is said that it is the supreme among all letters because it is natural. It is spontaneously self-arisen. It is not produced or contrived in any way. For example, it is the first sound made by a baby. Therefore, it is said to be unborn. As unborn, it is the symbol of emptiness itself. "AH" signifies Mahasunyata[6]. It is called the king of all letters. Just as the letter AH pervades all the other letters of the alphabet, so emptiness pervades all other phenomena. It is the underlying substratum of reality. The letter AH personifies emptiness. First, you dissolve everything into emptiness, which means to abandon your view of yourself, companions, and your environment as being ordinary. When you practice the developing stage of deity yoga, according to tantric procedure, you need to

---

[6] Literally: 'Great Emptiness'

let go of ordinary, demeaning, limited perception, and cultivate pure view. Not seeing you and others as flesh and blood (ordinary beings), but rather as Chenrezig. Not seeing this building, as an ordinary building, rather seeing it as a celestial mansion in the midst of the Pureland of Great Bliss. The Lama is not an ordinary teacher, but is in fact the true manifestation of the Buddha Amitabha. This is called the 'cultivation of the exalted view of the developing stage'. The next line says, "All phenomena, all experiences are unborn". They are pervaded by emptiness, just as the letters of the alphabet are pervaded by AH. The next line says, "This is the nature of reality." The natural condition is great compassion and awareness of emptiness, non-dual. This is not something fabricated by the mind. This not just our idea, this is not something we create by thinking it so. It is the essential nature of reality itself. It is now, has always been, will always be the case that emptiness and compassion are the ultimate nature of reality.

The next line on page three, that begins with 'Kung Nan Rig Ped Chung Tro Ley', means that all-pervading, substratum of reality. The true nature of existence, which is compassion and emptiness, is not dormant. Just as the sun naturally emanates its rays resulting in illumination, the nature of reality manifests from the unmanifest Dharmakaya the rays of compassion and wisdom radiating into our realm of existence. The manifestation takes the symbolic form of a lotus blossom, upon which is a moon seat. The lotus blossom signifies freedom from defilement. The moon seat signifies being free from attachment or desire. They both signify the white seed of the father and the red seed of the mother. The birth of a human being in our realm takes place when the white thig'le (bindu) of the father and the red thig'le of the mother come together and between them is the consciousness of the being to be born. When those three factors come together, a being is born in this world. What is symbolically presented here is rebirth into the Pure Realm of Pure Perception of the Developing Stage of Deity Yoga. In the Pureland, birth takes place in a similar way. The lotus symbolizes the red seed of the mother, and the moon seat symbolizes the white seed of the father. One's own consciousness is between them. One then abandons the ordinary view and develops divine view. Because of that, one is born in the form of Chenrezig, having one face and four hands. The essence of the procedure of the Developing Stage of Deity Yoga is as follows. In our ordinary view we are engaged in what we consider worship: we think of the deity as something external and then offer various substances and ourselves as a service to that deity. In the Developing Stage of Deity Yoga, the procedure is different. One eliminates the view of oneself, one's environment, and one's companions in this world as ordinary. If you see yourself as an ordinary human being, then your mind is under the sway of the virulence of the five poisons[7]. To eliminate the five poisons, one cultivates the divine view. One sees one's self, his environment, and companions as divine. The cultivation of the divine view effectively removes the five poisons from one's mindstream. If you are Chenrezig, and not an ordinary flesh and blood human being, if you are the Bodhisattva of Boundless compassion, then you have no ignorance, attachment,

---

[7] Ignorance, attachment, aversion, pride, and jealousy

aversion, pride, or jealousy. You mindstream is then, innately and primordially pure. That innate primordial purity is cultivated in the divine vision of the Developing Stage of Deity Yoga. Another reason for the cultivation of the divine view is that if you cultivate the qualities of the Buddha, by considering them you're own, then, little by little, they become your own qualities. The more you contemplate possessing these qualities, the more they actually increase. By slow stages, you develop the qualities of the enlightened being. On the other hand, the more you develop these qualities, the more you abandon negative qualities and mindsets. Little by little, your negativity is lessened and the positive nature of your mind manifests. Just as when the sun rises, little by little the darkness disperses. That process takes place simultaneously. The more the light increases the more the darkness decreases. The more you contemplate the qualities of enlightenment, the more you develop those qualities, and the more your limitations are overcome. To symbolize the completion of great compassion in the form of Chenrezig, one meditates on one's own body color as being a luminescent white (moon like) color. Your have one face and four hands, In the first hand, the upper right hand, you hold a crystal mala, symbolizing the capacity to liberate all sentient beings from cyclic existence. The upper left hand holds the stem of the lotus blossom. The lotus blossom is a flower that is rooted in muck and yet grows and blossoms above it in a way that is pure. The flower is in no way stained or defiled by the muck and mire in which it is rooted. This is symbolic of the fact that although as human beings we have fallen into cyclic existence, and abides within it. Yet, we have within us the inalienable core of our being our actual original nature and it is enlightened (tathagarba[8]). That Buddha-nature is in no way defiled by the apparent stains of cyclic existence. The first pair of hands a folded in the prayer mudra in front of Chenrezig at His heart level. The gesture is quite elegant. The hands are cupping the Wish Fulfilling Jewel[9]. The Wish Fulfilling Jewel is symbolic of Chenrezig's power to liberate all sentient beings from suffering. The next line says that Chenrezig appears in the form of Samboghakaya[10]. In that form, he appears as an enlightened being manifesting in the body of visionary enjoyment. He wears various ornaments. There are three different groups of ornamentation. For example, there are five types of silk garments, the silk that holds together the jewels of the crown, a shawl, a skirt, a belt (or sash), and a long flowing scarf. There are eight types of jewel ornaments. The jewels in the crown are earrings, a choker necklace, a longer necklace that hangs to the heart chakra, an even longer necklace that hangs to the navel, arm bands, bracelets on the wrists and ankles, and finally, rings. These are always present in all Samboghakaya forms. His two legs (your two legs) are crossed in the full lotus position. You then meditate on that appearance with great clarity and sense of reality. However, it is not a flesh and blood construct. Rather,

---

[8] Sanskrit word for Buddha-nature

[9] In the West, we might say the 'Philosopher's stone'.

[10] In this sadhana, Amitabha Buddha, the Buddha of Boundless Light, is the Nirmanakaya, the manifest self-referential. Amitabha Buddha is adorned like Shakyamuni Buddha in the three types of robes of a monk.

it is an empty, self-luminous form, devoid of self-nature, yet appearing in exact detail. Remember that you are visualizing yourself as Chenrezig. In the space in front of you facing you, appears Amitabha Buddha. He is seated upon a throne held aloft by eight peacocks[11], two in each corner of the throne. On top of the throne is a variegated one thousand petaled lotus blossom. On top of the lotus blossom is a moon seat. The moon seat symbolizes the assuaging of the fiery nature of delusion and afflictions. The cool rays of the moon seat calm that down. On top of the moon disk seat, standing upright is the essence of Amitabha Buddha, the syllable HRIH. It is red in color. Amitabha Buddha appears from the transformation of the letter HRIH. Amitabha Buddha is the representative of all the Buddhas of the ten directions and the three times. He is deep ruby red in body color. He has one face and two hands. His hands rest in Dhyana Mudra[12] form. His feet are in the full lotus position. He holds in his hands a begging bowl filled with the nectar of immortality. To His right is Chenrezig. To his left is Vajrapani[13]. Normally Vajrapani is very wrathful looking; here he is not like that. He is portrayed in a peaceful form or manifestation. Both Chenrezig and Vajrapani are standing and they are slightly turned toward Amitabha Buddha. They each have one face and two hands. They stand on top of sun and moon disks. The complete congregation of enlightened beings such as bodhisattvas and arhats surrounds them. Let us recap

---

[11] The peacocks symbolize the freedom from desire.

[12] The gesture of meditative equipoise

[13] Known as the 'Lord of Powerful Means', Vajrapani is one of the Eight Mahabodhisattvas.

41

for a moment. You are Chenrezig. In the space in front of you is Amitabha Buddha. To His right is Chenrezig and to His left is Vajrapani. They are surrounded by the mandala of all enlightened beings. From the crown, throat, and heart chakras of the three central figures, light rays emanate white, red, and blue. Those light rays constitute an invitation to the wisdom beings in their Purelands to come forth and join with the commitment beings, which have been created by the visualization. This is called an Invitation. The wisdom beings come forth and descend like downpour of light bodies in the form of Amitabha Buddha, Chenrezig, and Vajrapani. They come forth from the Pureland and merge with the visualized construct collectively known as the commitment being. At the bottom of page seven, it is written: "Hung Hrih, from the realm of Dewachen in the west. Oh Lord Amitabha! Please be on this stainless throne of lotus, sun, and moon disks." That is called the invitation. The second thing that happens here is having invited Him, You invite Him to take a seat on the throne prepared for Him. Amitabha Buddha then takes His seat and you make obeisance to Him. You prostrate to Him with your body, speech, and mind. Then you make offerings to Him. This is not a set of ordinary offerings. Instead, you offer all the elements of existence to Him. Having done that, you begin to have a heart to heart conversation with Amitabha Buddha. In this case, you confess to Him all your downfalls and broken vows. You open your heart to Amitabha Buddha in that way. The wisdom beings have come and hovered over the assembly of commitment beings, they are still visualized as external to you as Chenrezig. You tell them to sit down and accept the offerings, and then you confess your non-virtues. They will dissolve into the commitment being (visualized as Amitabha Buddha, Chenrezig, and Vajrapani) at the recitation of the mantra Za Hung Bam Ho[14]. (Here, His Holiness takes some time to demonstrate the mudra that goes with saying of the mantra.) We come, now, to the part of the sadhana that constitutes the recitation of the mantra. Having merged the wisdom beings with the commitment beings, in the heart of Buddha Amitabha on top of a lotus and moon disk (lying flat), is the seed syllable Hrih, standing upright. The letters of the mantra 'Om Ami Dewa Hrih' are set up on the edge of the moon disk. They are set up counterclockwise, but rotate clockwise. As you recite the mantra, light rays emanate from the mantric syllables and transform the whole universe as an external container into the Pureland of Great Bliss. In addition, with all sentient beings as the contents of that container, transform into the commitment being. While reciting the mantra, you hold the idea that the experience of what is called 'The Three Vajras': Vajra body, Vajra speech, and Vajra mind. That is to say, all form is the enlightened body of Amitabha Buddha, all sound is the mantra of Amitabha Buddha, and all thought is the movement of Amitabha Buddha's consciousness. With that realization, your recite the mantra 'Om Ami Dewa Hrih.'

---

[14] Za Hung means 'please stay'. That brings the wisdom beings forth and they remain. They come to a point above the head of commitment being. Then they dissolve into it. Bam means they become non-dual. Ho means the process has taken place and you rejoice in that fact.

(At this point, His Holiness leads His students in the practice of the sadhana up until the recitation of the mantra.)

When you begin to recite the mantra, you should visualize light rays boundlessly emanating from the commitment being in front of you. First, offer the light to the enlightened beings of the ten directions, then the light comes back to emanate once more to touch and purify all sentient beings. You recite the mantra for as long as you have time, or for a set number of repetitions.

As the practice winds down, you visualize that light rays emanating from the commitment being. The light rays dissolve the external environment into the three main figures of the commitment being. Then, Chenrezig and Vajrapani dissolve into Amitabha Buddha. From Amitabha's four places, the crown, throat, heart, and navel chakras, light rays[15] emanate and strike you in the four corresponding places. This cleanses and purifies you from all obscurations of body, speech, and mind. The light rays transfer to you the four empowerments. The Amitabha Buddha melts into light and dissolves into you through the point between the eyebrows. At this point, you enter the inseparability of emptiness and appearance. You allow the mind to rest in its own natural sphere, the state of Mahamudra.

What has gone on up to now has to do with the developing stage practice of the deity yoga of Amitabha Buddha. Everything that is concerned with the

---

[15] The corresponding colors of these light rays are white, red, blue, and yellow.

44

developing stage practice has a particular point of reference. It has an object of meditation, a support of meditation. When Amitabha Buddha dissolves into light and merges with you, you enter what is called the Completion Stage practice of the Deity Yoga of Amitabha Buddha. In this stage, there is no fixed frame of reference. This is a state beyond thought. A state transcends the conceptual mind. The purpose of the practice of the Developing Stage of Deity Yoga is to overcome one's view of oneself and one's surroundings as ordinary. It is to make divine your view of existence itself. It is to overcome your attachment to an ordinary, demeaning view. The purpose of the completion stage practice is to overcome your view of your self and your environment as divine. Therefore, having attained the beatific vision, you go beyond the beatific vision by giving up your attachment to this divine view. It is said that the developing stage practice perfects the accumulation of merit, and the completion stage practice perfects the accumulation of wisdom. Both practices taken together in fact, are an inseparable unity, yield Buddhahood. This practice combines, in a quintessential way, the main practices of sutra and tantra. This is a non-dual practice of sutra and tantra leading to non-dual realization, and non-dual accumulation of wisdom and merit.

Teachings on Vajrakilaya[16]

This afternoon His Holiness is going to bestow the
empowerment of Vajrakilaya. For people who are new
to the process of empowerment you should know that
you will be given a drink of water. You take the water in
your cupped hands, with the left hand on top of the
right hand. Then sip it and swirl it in your mouth. At
the time, you drink this water; you should visualize and
experience all your obscurations and negativities as
purified by this water. This way you enter the precincts
of this empowerment as purified. What happens now is
that a torma, a ritual cake made of parched barley flour
is offered up to all the countervailing forces that might
hover around the area of the initiation. This means
either human or non-human obstructers. They are
offered the cake as a symbol of whatever they need or
want. Thereby they become satiated and filled. The
torma is offered not only offered in a simple way, with
mantra, mudra, and samadhi. When the torma is
offered, the obstructers rejoice and depart. In
Vajrayana Buddhism, this is done in a way that seems
external. What it symbolizes is that it is one's own
mindsets that are contaminated by anger, aversion, or
hatred is pacified. Thereby no obstructions will arise
during the empowerment. In requesting and entering
the empowerment mandala of Vajrakilaya, you should
set your motivation, first and foremost, as being not
just for yourself, but in order to gain the capacity to
liberate all sentient beings. Let your altruistic
aspiration be the liberation of all sentient beings from

---

[16] In Tibetan: Dorje Phurba.

their sufferings. The process you are about to experience is called empowerment, or initiation[17]. It is a key element to the practices of Vajrayana Buddhism. The initiation is necessary to practice. Just as perfume essences are ground from various substances and made into oils, if they are not ground and made into oils there will be no scent. A master who has received the empowerment himself from an intact lineage must transmit empowerment. Here the lineage that Rinpoche received, and from which He is transmitting the empowerment to us today, is without break. Specifically, His Holiness received this empowerment and the permission to transmit it from the lineage of Ratna Lingpa, who was a great treasure discoverer of Dorje Phurba. Later he received the oral transmission and teachings from Kyabjé Dilgo Khyentse Rinpoche. Empowerment is an extremely important matter. It is crucial. Without empowerment, you will not have the power to practice. If you attempt to practice and you practice incorrectly, it will only lead to negative experiences. It is said you can end up in the hell realms if you practice without proper empowerment. You need to take this quite seriously because the empowerment is a transmission to you from an intact lineage and you need to keep it intact. If you break the lineage of practice, then the vajra master himself is subject to rebirth in the hell realms. In Tibetan, the word for empowerment literally means power. What kind of power are we speaking of? We are speaking of the kind of power a king has. The authority of a king is a very powerful thing. When you attain empowerment, it means you receive the authority as an edict, like from a

---

[17] In Tibetan: 'wang'.

king, to do the practice. Today you are receiving the empowerment of Vajrakilaya; establishing a relationship with him and if you practice you will gain the power of His accomplishment. In Sanskrit, the word for empowerment is abhisheka. 'Abi' means everything that is offered, sacrificed, or done away with. In the process of empowerment, you should think that 'abi' means that you do away with, or sacrifice, the five poisons (ignorance, attachment, aversion, jealousy, and arrogance). They are gone! Driven away from you. 'Sheka' means that you are consecrated. There are four different empowerment processes that take place. The first is called the vase empowerment. In that, you are given some water, which you should consider to be wisdom nectar of Vajrakilaya. It enters into you through the crown of your head. Then you successively receive the consecration as it moves down, activating the centers of power in your yogic body. Therefore, when it comes to the crown, you receive the first empowerment, the empowerment of the vase. When the wisdom nectar arrives at the throat, you receive the second empowerment, which is called the 'secret' empowerment[18]. Then the nectar goes to the heart center and you receive the empowerment of 'discriminating wisdom of primordial awareness'. At the navel, the fourth center, you receive the empowerment of non-duality, the non-dual essence of awareness and emptiness, which is called the 'Great Seal', or 'Mahamudra'. The process of initiation is a ripening of your mindstream. Just as a fruit becomes ripe, so your own mindstream can ripen. Your own mental continuum is brought to fruition through this

---

[18] It is the empowerment of speech, the secret mantra.

process. Buddhahood is gained through the process of ripening. The seeds are planted for that gaining of Buddhahood. When you receive the vase empowerment, it is the cleansing of all the negativities of you body and the planting of the seed of Nirmanakaya, the manifestation of enlightened consciousness. When you receive the secret empowerment, it is the purification of all the obscurations of speech and vibrational patterns. That plants the seed for the eventual realization of Samboghakaya, the body of visionary enjoyment perceivable by advanced adepts of enlightened consciousness. When you receive the third empowerment, the empowerment of primordial awareness, it is the purification of all obscuration of your mind. It plants the seed for the eventual realization of the dharmakaya, the unmanifest self-referential state of enlightened consciousness. When you receive the fourth empowerment, it is the purification of all the obscurations of body, speech, and mind together. It is the planting of the seed for the eventual realization of the essential body of awareness, combining all other modes of manifestation. It is called, in Sanskrit, the Svabavikakaya, which means the essential body (or manifestation) of enlightened consciousness. The fourth empowerment is especially important you should pay attention to it. It is, if you understand it, the transmission of the enlightened state of Mahamudra (the Great Seal). It is the complete and utter manifestation of the nature reality just as it is. The origin of the lineage of the transmission of the empowerment of Vajrakilaya is from Kuntunzangpo[19].

---

[19] In Sanskrit: Samantabhadra.

From Samantabhadra, the manifestation of Vajrakilaya appeared as Vajrakumara, the youthful wrathful form of Vajrakilaya. It was transmitted to eight great Vidhyadaras[20]. It eventually came down to Guru Padmasambhava. Guru Rinpoche taught it in Tibet in various places and also practiced the realization of Vajrakilaya in Nepal at Jang Re Shal, which is a great cave. Then the treasure of Vajrakilaya was hidden away and discovered in various forms by different treasure discoverers, called Tertöns, over generations, and it has come down in an unbroken lineage to His Holiness. The empowerment granted today is the essence of all the Tertöns derived from Guru Padmasambhava. Specifically, Padmasambhava gave this empowerment, in Tibet, to the king Tetson Detsen and his main disciples. This lineage is a treasure lineage. There are three kinds of treasures, earth, sky, and mind treasures. This is an earth treasure. A Terton named Ösel Dorje took it out of the earth in a particular place[21]. He was a previous incarnation of Dilgo Khyentse Rinpoche. This treasure bears the style of Dilgo Khyentse Rinpoche. There are many treasures floating about Tibet and some are authoritative. This one is quite authoritative because it bears the stamp of Dilgo Khyentse Rinpoche. In order to receive the empowerment, it is necessary to ask the Vajra Master to bestow the empowerment. Now we will repeat a request prayer asking the Vajra Master give the empowerment.

---

[20] Holders of the lineage
[21] The name means "Adamantine Light Rays."

At this point His Holiness starts the empowerment ceremony with the request prayer[22]...

(The teachings continue in the evening.)

I am now going to teach the practice (sadhana) of Dorje Phurba stage by stage. The first part of the Sadhana of Vajrakilaya is taking refuge. You take refuge in the Enlightened Beings of the Three Times. You take refuge in all the Buddhas, Bodhisattvas, Lamas, and enlightened beings currently in this world with unwavering intent. Imagine here, that your own lama is Vajrakilaya subsuming all the Buddhas of the Three Times. You should understand that your teacher is the enlightened form of Vajrakilaya in this world. The second part of the sadhana is the generation of bodhicitta. In general, this is true of all sadhanas. Taking refuge and generating bodhicitta go together as a unified, synchronistic pattern of energy counteracting the energy of ignorance, or primitive beliefs concerning the nature of reality. The third part is the establishment of boundaries. We say here "All those inimical, countervailing spiritual forces who would militate against the accomplishment of our practice, we cut you off! We lay down the boundary here you cannot come in!" What does this mean? It means our own thoughts, our own negative mindsets, which are not an actual part of the nature of reality. We cut them off. We lay them aside. We draw a line in the sand. With outer, inner, and secret offerings, we make boundaries with

---

[22]As this is only for the eyes and ears of the attendees of the empowerment, I will resume the transcription of the commentary, after the initiation.

52

body speech and mind, which cannot be violated. Let go. Completely dissolve your view of yourself and your surroundings as ordinary. Dissolve into the sphere of great emptiness. From emptiness arises the letter 'Hung'. From the letter 'Hung' arises a lotus and sun disk seat radiating light. Its essence is empty. Its nature is cognitively charged and luminously aware. Its wisdom energy is all-pervasive. It manifests in an unimpeded manner. The entire outer universe arises from it, and the entire inner universe, namely the sentient beings resident in the outer universe, arises from it as well. The four great elements of earth, air, fire, and water all come from it. It manifests as a boundless celestial mansion. The boundless celestial mansion is square. It has four corners. It is boundless, yet it has four corners. In the center, arises the letter 'Eh' above it. From the instantaneous transformation of the letter, 'Eh' arises a wheel with ten spokes, representing the ten directions[23]. From the wheel, arise a lotus and sun seat. On top of the lotus and sun seat there appears the upstanding letter 'Hung'; from the instantaneous transformation of which arises Vajrakilaya. One visualizes, then, the true presence of Vajrakilaya in the following manner: He appears having three faces and six hands. On the crown of his head is the tiara, which encompasses the Buddhas of the Five Families. He represents the full manifestation of the four bodies of enlightenment (Dharmakaya, Samboghakaya, Nirmanakaya, and Svavabhikakaya). He

---

[23] The eight cardinal directions plus the zenith and the nadir

has in his five places[24]the syllables 'Om', 'Tam', 'Hung', 'Hrih', and 'Ah'. He represents the self-awareness and the spontaneous self-arisen presence of all manifestations of enlightened consciousness in and of himself.

At this point in the sadhana, one performs offerings. One offers to Vajrakilaya[25] water for the mouth, water for the feet, perfume and incense, the light of candles, flowers to delight the senses, food, and sound. Those are the outer offerings; the inner offerings are blood and semen[26]. After the offerings are made, there is a stanza of praise: "I myself am Vajrakilaya. In myself as Vajrakilaya, at the center of my heart, is another Vajrakilaya (standing upright and the size of my thumb), and in the heart center of that Vajrakilaya, standing upright, is a vajra in the navel of which is the letter 'Hung'". Around the letter 'Hung', are the letters of the mantra. These letters are setup counterclockwise, but rotating clockwise. 'Om' is in the front, then 'Vajra, Kili, Kilaya, Sarwa, Bigana, Bam, Hung, Phat' as you recite the mantra. As one recites the mantra, light rays emanate out. The tendered offerings to the enlightened beings come back and radiate out again and touch all sentient beings, healing them, bringing them into the teachings of Dharma. Then all the light rays emanate and purify the four elements that constitute constituent

---

[24] That means the crown, throat, heart, navel, and secret chakras.
[25] These are offerings made to the old kings in ancient India. When kings returned to their palaces they were given these offerings.
[26] Blood and semen are the essence of female and male energy.

being. The light rays go out again and make offerings to all the enlightened beings. Then the light dissolves into oneself as Vajrakilaya. There is nothing other than that. That is the visualization and the mindset to hold while reciting the mantra. You recite the mantra as much as you can. While reciting the mantra, the four activities of enlightened consciousness are enacted. That means luring, enriching, magnetizing, and destroying, whatever needs to be done is enacted. Other than that, there is no purpose to mantras. His Holiness then leads the practitioners into the practice of the mantra....

Seeing one's self as Vajrakilaya, while reciting the mantra, hold on to the view of yourself as the yidam. In your heart center is the wisdom being Vajrakilaya. From the 'Hung' in his heart center light rays radiate out and penetrate the ten directions of space. Then make offerings to all the enlightened beings, and heal and purify the stains and defilements of all sentient beings. Eliminate the limitations of all sentient beings. The light rays then return in to you. All that is conceived as 'outer world' dissolves into the central figures of the visualization: oneself as Vajrakilaya. Then the whole divine realm of Vajrakilaya dissolves into Vajrakilaya himself. Vajrakilaya dissolves into the being at his heart. The being at dissolves into the letter 'Hung'. The letter 'Hung' dissolves from the bottom up until it enters into the sphere of emptiness where there is no reference point, no 'inside', no 'outside', no 'other', no subject, no object, and you allow the mind to subside into and rest within its own sphere, in that realization of non-dual awareness and emptiness. As long as you are able, you allow the mind to reside within its own natural sphere. Then, thoughts, specifiable appearances, and experiences begin to arise again. You let them arise as the letter 'Hung', which instantaneously transforms into the appearance of Vajrakilaya. At his crown center is the white letter 'Om', at his throat center is the red letter 'Ah', and at his heart center is the blue letter 'Hung'. Light rays emanate out and penetrate the ten directions of space. You hold to the realization that all form is the manifestation of Vajrakilaya. All sound is the manifestation of the mantra. All thought is the movement of Vajrakilaya's enlightened consciousness. In that realization, you dedicate the merit, or the positive energy accumulated in the practice of the sadhana to the welfare of all sentient beings. That concludes the empowerment and a brief teaching of how to practice the sadhana of Vajrakilaya.

Oral Commentaries on the Heart Sutra in relation to Shamatha and Vipassana Meditation

And

Seven Point Mind Training

By

His Eminence

Garchen Rinpoche

San Francisco, September 2001

Translated by Robert Clarke
Transcribed and Edited by Jeffery A. Beach

Introduction

I could not have been more fortunate in my decision to transcribe the recording of these oral commentaries of His Eminence Garchen Rinpoche, which took place in San Francisco during the last week of September 2001. The laborious process has been a transforming one. I never expected to be so impacted by these teachings. Transcribing and editing became part of my daily practice. It is a wonderful thing to decelerate and write down tape recordings of teachings because it gives one no choice but to be attentive, especially since my style of typing is of the hunt and peck variety. The editing process made me contemplate the text in a slow deliberate way. It is not like reading a book the way I normally would. I remember someone telling me a long time ago that Khenchen Könchog Gyaltshen Rinpoche remarked one day that to properly read and understand a book, one should read it at least thirty or forty times. The process of transcribing and editing a text is somewhat like that. I have always wondered how to properly, and completely integrate the Eightfold Path, and the Six Paramitas into my daily life, I needed a good roadmap and immediately found Seven Point Mind Training to be just that.

In all humility, I personally recommend this process to all Dharma centers. It is important to undertake similar projects with the recordings of dharma teachings, because they are veritable treasures, and they should not be gathering dust. The transcriptions of recordings are important for future generations when long after the passing of present teachers their light will still shine. In this era of computers, Internet, and books on demand, the cost of publishing has declined to the point that it is an affordable undertaking. It is an excellent fundraising tool as well.

A word about the editing process, I tried to stay as true to the original tape recordings of the teachings, as possible. I felt my main duty was to correct grammatical errors and usage for readability, as text has a different flavor than listening to a translation at a teaching.

The Heart Sutra Commentaries

To begin with, Rinpoche says, "Welcome" to all his Dharma friends. We will begin by reading the Heart Sutra. Rinpoche says this is not something in which he is very learned. He received the transmission of the text, however, explaining all its details and particularities is not possible in the short amount of time we have. Some things he knows, and some he does not. Those he knows he will share with us.

The Buddha gave this teaching on Prajñaparamita at Vulture Peak in the kingdom of Jattrashatru, near the capital city. He taught the sutra to the assembly of monks and the great assembly of Bodhisattvas.

The first line of the text says: "I pay homage to the all-knowing Prajñaparamita". As the Prajñaparamita is the very essence of all the Buddha's teachings, paying homage to the Prajñaparamita is the equivalent to paying homage to all of the 84,000 sections of the Lord Buddha's Teachings. It is important to understand the terms of this sutra, as this is an essence teaching, each term has great significance.

The first word 'Bhagavati', means the 'The All-Victorious One'. It is the defining term of the Prajñaparamita. It is the 'All-Conquering Prajñaparamita'. What does it conquer? It says in the text that it is called the 'All-Conquering', because it completely overcomes and vanquishes the Four Maras. The Four Maras are the Mara of the skandhas, the Mara of the kleshas, the Mara of death, and the divine Mara. Included in the Four Maras are all the obstacles to perfect enlightenment, and the Prajñaparamita conquers them all.

The term 'Bhagavati', not only expresses the ability to conquer, it also means that which conquers through wisdom. What is this wisdom spoken of here? It is the wisdom, which encompasses all good qualities. The Prajñaparamita has all of the qualities of wisdom overcomes the Four Maras, and attains the state of the three bodies: Dharmakaya (Limitless as the Sky), Samboghakaya (The Perfect Transcendent Body), and Nirmanakaya (the Manifestation Body). Through the three bodies, the possibility of liberating all living beings, without exception, exists.

The term 'Bhagavati' in Tibetan is 'Chom Den Dey'. Each of these syllables has meaning. 'Chom' means the 'conquering aspect of the Maras'; the second syllable 'Den' means 'to possess the qualities of perfect wisdom', which brings about the three bodies. The fourth syllable 'Dey', means to 'transcend all of Samsara and Nirvana', in other words, both the ordinary world, and the solitary Nirvana.

Understanding the Prajñaparamita, one obtains the non-abiding nirvana, the state of full transcendence; transcending all mental afflictions, together with their latencies. The next syllable in the Tibetan text is 'Ma'. 'Ma' is the feminine ending, and it means that this Bhagavati, the Prajñaparamita, is the source, the mother of all the Buddhas, past, present, and future. It is because of the Prajñaparamita, that they attain the state of highest enlightenment, and become Buddhas. The Prajñaparamita is the Mother of all Buddhas.

The second word of the text is 'Prajñaparamita'. The first part of the word is 'Prajña', or 'Sherab' in Tibetan. 'Sherab' has two general meanings. The first is what we call 'worldly wisdom', the wisdom of ordinary worldly discernment, where you discern things, and figure them out. This is what we call empirical thinking, or analysis. The second meaning is transcendent wisdom. This is the wisdom whereby realizing the way to free yourself from Samsara, with all its miseries, you attain the state of liberation and Buddhahood.

Wisdom in this instance has three aspects. There is the wisdom arising from hearing and studying, the wisdom arising from contemplation, and the wisdom arising from meditation. These wisdoms develop consecutively. You cultivate the first one first, then from that, the second arises, then from accomplishing the second, the ability to do the third arises.

The term 'Para' in Prajñaparamita, or 'Parol' in Tibetan, means 'beyond', or 'other side of'. What is one getting beyond? It is the getting beyond the appearance of all phenomena. Phenomena that appear to us do not exist in the way that they appear. Therefore, we have to get beyond appearance, the superficial appearance of objects, and beyond the two extremes of existence and non-existence. Getting beyond those extremes, we can come to see things as they actually are.

The other meaning of the term 'para' is that through understanding the Prajñaparamita, one sees beyond birth and death. The nature of the mind is beyond birth and death. Because of our own ignorance, we do not realize it and continually entangle ourselves in birth and death. Through the Prajñaparamita, we overcome and eliminate ignorance, and realize transcendence over birth and death.

The next term, 'hydraya', in Sanskrit, and 'nyingbo' in Tibetan, means 'heart'. The reason for calling this the 'heart' of the Prajñaparamita is that just as the

63

Prajñaparamita is the heart, or the soul of all Buddhist teachings, this text is the heart of the Prajñaparamita. It sums up in very few verses the entire teaching of the Prajñaparamita.

The next term is 'Chag Sal Lo' in Tibetan, meaning 'I bow down to' the Prajñaparamita. 'Bow down' is the term normally used for bowing down to the Buddha. Because the Prajñaparamita is the mother of all the Buddhas, and the essence of all of the Buddha's teachings, then, bowing down to the Prajñaparamita is the equivalent to bowing down to all of the Buddhas, and to all the teachings.

We pay verbal and physical homage, but the aspect of mental homage is most important. Mental homage is the honor one pays through understanding the text. The understanding of the meaning of Prajñaparamita comes by way of seven different specifics. The first of these is the introductory aspect of the text itself, and entering into its conveyed wisdom. Next, is the definition of emptiness, then the sphere of activity of wisdom, and then there are the qualities of wisdom, and the results of the mantra of wisdom.

Next in the text is the description of the 'entrance into wisdom', or the coming to understand wisdom. The text describes it as the Lord Buddha going into a profound meditative state out of his unlimited compassion. He focused on the ultimate nature of all things. Then, through the power of his samadhi, and his profound meditation, He inspired his disciple Sariputra to ask Arya Avalokiteshvara, also inspired by the Buddha's meditation, to answer Sariputra's question.

The question asked how it was that those who came to understand the profound emptiness as taught by the

Prajñaparamita, came to that realization. In other words, how should those who wish to understand the Prajñaparamita, proceed?

Avalokiteshvara explains it to the assembly. He says that the five aggregates, in and of themselves, are empty of reality.

The first of the aggregates is form. How do we understand form as empty? Form is empty because it is like a bubble. A bubble has shape. It appears and looks like something, but it is very insubstantial. You can understand the first type. The physical body is like a bubble, the kind of bubble you get in milk. It has the ability to stay a while, yet it is not very substantial. If you try to squeeze it, it pops, and disappears.

The second aggregate, the feeling aggregate, is like a bubble of water, which is very unstable. It appears, you can see it, but it goes away just as fast. It has no ability to stay, or hold its shape.

The third aggregate is the aggregate of discriminative functions. For instance, when you see some food, you can identify it as something to eat. However, it is like a mirage, it does not have any existence at all.

The fourth aggregate is the aggregate of compositional factors. It is like a hollow reed. A hollow reed grows and looks solid, but it is hollow.

The fifth aggregate is consciousness. Consciousness is like an illusion, but this illusion is not the same as a mirage. A mirage is a visual illusion. Whereas consciousness is an illusion in which we completely enmesh ourselves. We fall for it, and we think it is something real. It is an ongoing illusion. We have a feeling that there is some substantial 'I', or 'self' from this illusion of consciousness over a period of time, but just like any illusion, it is not real. When we look for it, we will not find it.

We should keep in mind that the Lord Buddha inspired this dialogue between Sariputra and Avalokiteshvara. 'Inspired' means that Lord Buddha, in his profound meditation, gave Sariputra the power to ask that key question. He also gave Avalokiteshvara the power to answer it. In other words, the Heart Sutra is coming from the power of the mind of the Enlightened One.

The way Sariputra phrases the question is that he asks how a man or woman, having attained this Buddha's lineage (literally called 'The Good Nature'[27]), and who desires to follow this profound path of Prajñaparamita, should come to understand this teaching. Avalokiteshvara's answer discusses the nature of the five aggregates. The aggregates are that which make up a sentient being. These aggregates are empty. They are empty of true existence. They nominally exist, but they lack inherent existence. Thus, in that way they are insubstantial, like a mirage, or an illusion, appearing and functioning, but lacking anything behind them. This is the essence of the teaching on emptiness; that is to say, it is the ultimate truth of all things. Avalokiteshvara is not saying that they do not exist. What he is saying is that they do not inherently exist. This is a profound distinction. By believing that aggregates inherently exist, that they exist of and by themselves, independent of anything else, we immerse

---

[27] "The Good Nature" means those of the Mahayana lineage, and who have the good fortune to follow the Mahayana Teachings.

into the illusion, and suffer all of the consequences of the entanglements of the cycle of birth and death.

The definition that marks the nature of emptiness is understood by the way it relates to all other aspects of phenomena. The definition of emptiness takes notice of the way it is related to all other aspects of phenomena. The first aggregate, form, is empty, and emptiness is form. You should not think of emptiness as something that exists in some way apart from form. Nor should you think that form has true existence. You should understand that form is empty. Any form is empty of unique, independent, and inherent existence.

The problem is that forms appear to inherently exist. Therefore, we form attachments to some, and aversions to others. The prime example of that is our body. It has form, and we do not realize it to be empty. We think that there is something inherent there. We identify it as "me", or "mine", and we get much attached to it.

Then, there is also this feeling of attachment or aversion to other, and that gives rise to mental afflictions, like desire, hatred, pride, envy, and so forth. Because of those mental states, we act in ways that are harmful to ourselves, and others. Because we misperceive that things inherently exist, and do not realize the emptiness of form; emptiness itself is what appears continually to us.

Form and emptiness are not two different things when free from all clinging and illusion. Not only is form empty, and emptiness is form, it is the same case with each of the aggregates. The text says that "form is empty and emptiness is form and not something other than form, and form is not something other than emptiness. In the same way, feeling, discriminative functions, compositional factors, and consciousness are empty." All aspects of what we call reality, all phenomena, form (both internal and external), that we see arising in our experience, are empty. It is an all-inclusive list. All these things are empty and lack inherent existence.

When we realize this, then we can get rid of ignorance. What is ignorance? Ignorance is a type of consciousness. It is called 'the ignorant consciousness'. If we do not understand the Prajñaparamita, do not perfect wisdom, then our minds are of the 'ignorant variety'. We think: "I exist", "I am dying", clinging to the illusion of an 'I' that is inherently existent, and then we look about for some place to be reborn. We enter a womb, take up the aggregates again, and again take rebirth. This goes on and on until we realize the emptiness of the five aggregates.

Then, when one dies, there is no one who died, and there is no problem, do not think, "Oh, I have to have some rebirth." The mind of emptiness is realized, and the freedom from the cycle of birth and death achieved.

Next, Avalokiteshvara says to Sariputra: "In just this manner, all phenomena are empty." When he says 'all phenomena', this term means every thing; all of Samsara, nirvana, everything, there is nothing whatsoever which inherently exists. Nothing is held back here. There is no internal, external, or secret thing, which inherently exists. Existence is merely a mistake of conceptual thinking. It is fundamental ignorance to think that anything truly exists. The idea reinforced here is that all phenomena, without exception, are empty.

All things are empty in that they lack inherent identifiability. They are not produced and they do not cease. This means that the things that we perceive, appear to come into existence, and they appear to have some identifiable entity. However, if you look for it, you will not find it, because it is not there. If you look for something produced, you will not find it. There is the appearance of production, and the appearance of cessation.

However, any object, any thing that appears through dependent arising, that is to say, a cause and effect process, does not exist in and of itself. It is completely dependent on causes and conditions. There is no 'thing', no entity to be found. This process is the lack of any inherent existence in what is produced, and what ceases.

Defilement and the lack of defilement are the next things mentioned in the text. Normally we think of defilement as something we have to free the mind from, then we will clearly see what has to be realized, but the statement in the text says that ultimately there can be no defilement. It is like empty space. Empty space cannot be produced, and as it is not produced, it cannot cease. The nature of the mind is not different from that. It does not produce, nor does it cease. The true nature of mind, being the ultimate, it s not defiled, and therefore it cannot be freed from defilement.

For example, if you had some clothes you wish to clean, they, first, have to have some dirt on it. If the clothes are completely clean, you cannot clean them further. As the mind itself cannot inherently exist, then its defilements cannot inherently exist. There is a sense of duality, of subject and object, but this is illusory. There is no inherent duality of subject and object. Duality between the inner and outer is completely vacuous; therefore, there can be no defilements to purify. You can have neither defilement, nor freedom from defilement.

We should caution ourselves that perhaps, at this point we do not have Avalokiteshvara's understanding, or even that of Sariputra. When it is said that form is emptiness, and emptiness is form, we can, naturally, be very puzzled. We can think, "What is going on here? Obviously things exist, the body exists, those objects around me exist, and this sounds very strange." We then have to concede that if we are to understand this, it will take some work to reverse our usual way of perceiving things. Because we perceive things as if they truly, and naturally exist, and respond to them as such, that we create the world we know. We grasp things as existing in the way we perceive them. What that does, is to cause a whole stream of events, which become our karma, with one event leading to another. Conditioned existence, depending upon our ignorance, and on our karma, whether we will have a better, or worse, body or situation, or better or worse rebirth, depends upon this stream of cause and effect. The stream continually reinforces the illusion. When we stop and think about it, and that is what the meditation process is, we begin to see that things do not exist in the way we always thought. We can begin to free ourselves of those illusions and from the karma caused by those illusions. We should not think that we do not have any wisdom; we have wisdom. Wisdom is the ability to identify and discern. It is a very basic function. However, what we do not have is transcendent wisdom. This type of wisdom leads us to transcend the illusions of the world. It remains to be developed. It is something that can be developed. It is the wisdom that we have innately, and comes forth through meditative practice. It is a discriminative awareness that can identify things. We use the mind to develop it, and then we can identify more of our own nature, and inner reality and outer worlds. When we do not use our faculty of discriminative awareness, we assume things to be the way in which they appear. We respond to them incorrectly, involve ourselves more deeply into that process. Our physical body is evidence of that. It is the result of our ignorance, which assumes things to truly exist; it attaches to those things, and experiences them as pleasant, or unpleasant. Through that, we engage in activities, and take on a physical body. That physical body seems so truly real. You cannot believe that it does not, and assuming it is real, you accumulate karma, reinforcing the illusion. If you say: "Oh, everything is empty," then if someone hits and hurts you, you will normally respond with anger. That is the evidence of a strong misidentification to both the form and the feelings experienced. As we practice and cultivate an awareness of the meaning of emptiness, gradually we become freer of the illusions, and less attached to internal and external objects. The less we cling, the freer we become from illusion. Then we come to a point where we can understand what is meant by emptiness, The fact that we do have a basic wisdom, gives us to the ability to expand and develop that wisdom. We can come to point of perceiving emptiness, truly and directly. We ultimately become free from all illusions. Its proof is the nature of our own consciousness. Though consciousness lacks inherent existence, it is still what is called the 'tathagarba', meaning buddha-nature. Because we have awareness, that awareness can become sharper and sharper. We can learn to understand the true lack of inherent

71

existence in the nature of things; our awareness can overcome all illusion, and attain the state of perfect realization. When we practice meditation, even very briefly, we can have a moment, or two, of clear awareness, which can be continually developed, and expanded. As we free ourselves from the afflictive mental states, and develop what we already have, we are not gaining new awareness, some new mind; we are just manifesting what is already here. We have Prajñaparamita. We all have that fundamental Prajñaparamita, which is the nature of the clear or true nature of our ordinary mind. By practicing meditation, we become more aware of it, whereas our experience of it may be very brief, it can be expanded upon. Just like a small space is not different from space in general. If our awareness is like a small space, we are, then, very restricted and closed in; but through practice, the space gets bigger and bigger, becoming like the sky itself: unlimited. Tonight, you can go home and practice this, and tomorrow, you can say if you have realized Prajñaparamita, or not.

In the statement in the sutra where it says: "there is no defilement, no freedom from defilement, no decrease, and no increase," this and all other defining statements in the sutra, speak from the point of view of emptiness, from the point of view of the truth. There is no such thing as defilement, and as there is no defilement, there is no freedom from defilement. Again, as with the example of clothing, if your clothing is dirty, you can wash it. If the clothing is not dirty, there is nothing to wash. What about increasing or decreasing? In emptiness, there is no increase; there is no decrease. A vast ocean is not spoken of in terms of its increase or decrease. This is fundamental emptiness, as well as the ultimate nature of the Buddha, the Fully Enlightened One. That nature is not different from the true nature of all sentient beings. If you have the idea that the Buddha is one thing, sentient beings are another, you are mistaken. From the point of view of ultimate truth, there is nothing to distinguish them. They are both empty. The statements in the text govern the various aspects of phenomenal reality, all those things we believe to exist: physical form, feelings, discriminations, compositional factors, consciousness, all of the things which constitute ordinary reality, are gone over in the sutra, one by one, and the sutra says that these things do not inherently exist. Their appearance to us, and our belief in their existence, is the nature of an illusion. In fact, one can say that nothing whatsoever exists inherently, and leave it at that, but, because we have this long process of many lives of habituation in believing in these constituents, the sutra goes over them one by one. Another way you can understand this, is that if one of them does not exist, because of their interdependence, then nothing exists. For example, if the form of the tongue does not exist, there is no tongue. If there is no tongue, then there is no taste. Likewise, if the eye does not exist, external forms do not exist, and then there is no sight. Each thing depends on something else. If the subject does not exist, the object does not exist, and, accordingly, the sensations associated with them do not exist. The sutra goes over each of these in terms of the different organs of sense, as subject, their various objects, the act of sensing them, the identification of the discriminative aspects (for example, the eye identifies forms), and the compositional factors, which are the structures of these things giving them continuity, also don't exist, ultimately, or inherently. Consciousness cannot exist without any of those factors. As these things do not inherently exist, then why is it that we are so convinced that they do? In the next part of the text, it speaks of the mind as underlying all these things. In other words, the mind posits true existence to phenomena, this is fundamental ignorance, whereby the existence of objects is merely posited by thought and concept, and thought and concept are posited by the actions of the mind. That fundamental ignorance creates this illusory world. The text, next, goes into the twelve links of dependent arising. The first of these links is ignorance, but the sutra says there is no ignorance. The second link is compositional factors; again, the text says that there are no compositional factors, which means no karma. The sutra continues through the links to the twelfth, which is ageing and death, again, it says that there is no ageing or death. This is the way we can understand the cause and effect process. We start with fundamental ignorance, whose foundation is duality, the positing of a truly existent world. Once the world is posited, then there is desire and aversion towards those posited objects of the phenomenal world. Then, actions (karma) arise, which seek to interact with this phenomenal world, one action leading to another, going around the twelve links of dependent arising. In this way, the body, during each lifetime, takes on the further craving, grasping, becoming, birth, ageing, and death in the cycle of rebirth. The text says that, in fact, these do not exist in ultimate reality. Ignorance does not inherently exist; the result is that karma does not inherently exist. Next are the four truths: the truths of misery, cause, cessation, and the path. What define misery, are the afflictive mental states (kleshas), such as greed, anger, delusion, pride, and jealousy. They disturb the mind, and make it miserable by attachment and aversion. Although misery does not inherently exist, it is created by the mind. It comes from mental action. For example, when we have something that is dear to us, and we lose it, we experience misery, because we grasp at that happiness of possessing. It is that happiness, or rather that object of happiness, which does not inherently exist, and when it is gone, we experience misery. With the death of loved ones, great misery replaces the experience of happiness one experienced in their presence. Then, even though the loved ones are gone, perhaps long gone, when you think of them, you experience that misery again. It can be very painful, very powerful, because the mind itself creates the misery. Misery has no inherent existence. It only exists through the experience of mental creations. It is that way with all things, all misery. The mind creates misery through its grasping. Misery exists, even though it does not inherently exist. As with all things, we perceive them because it is the mind's function, through ignorance, to posit them. The cause of misery is defined as compulsive grasping. The third truth is cessation. Cessation is defined as the state of complete pacification of the mind. Cessation is the natural state. It is when you understand reality as it is, and you cease creating an illusory world. What separates us from understanding these teachings: being told that things do not exist, and why we still perceive them? This is where the fourth truth, the path, comes in. The path is the path of meditation, of Shamatha and Vipassana. Shamatha is the ultimate state of a perfectly focused mind, and Vipassana is the penetrating insight into reality. That is what takes us from merely hearing that things do not inherently exist, to actually realizing that. It is through the path of meditation that one becomes fully aware of ultimate reality. The text, here, says that there is no difference between sentient beings and Buddhas by stating: "there is no attainment, and no non-attainment." Because there is nothing to attain, how could there be any difference between ordinary sentient beings and Buddhas? If you think of empty space, you realize that it not something to grasp. You can search for it, and you will realize that it is right here. It has always been right here. There is nothing to grasp. There is nothing to take into your hand and put somewhere. The realization that there is nothing to attain is the attainment. When you speak of attaining Mahamudra, it is to understand that there is nothing whatsoever to realize, and that, is the realization. All things in Samsara, and nirvana, without exception, do not truly exist. It is all emptiness. If we look around us and see things that appear to exist, and we say, "where did this come from?" As we look at a vase, a vase with flowers, "where did this come from, who created this?" we start analyzing everything around us (Rinpoche pointing to his microphone), "who made this?" We are used to giving the more superficial answer, which is that it was made by hands, someone figured out how to make it, and put the little pieces together to make it. Did the hands do it themselves? No, in the case of the vase, or whatever we see around us that we say is fabricated, was really made by the mind. It was the mind that told the hands what to do. If you analyze every aspect of reality, you will find it was created by the mind. Everything, without exception, all aspects of reality, if you analyze it, was created by the mind. This

76

is analytical meditation, insight meditation, and together with Shamatha meditation, you can analyze all phenomena, and realize that they are mental creations. Their existence is posited by the mind. Then you turn that analytically focused meditation to the mind itself, sit in meditation, and start looking for the mind. Where did mind come from? What is the mind? You focus your meditation on the mind itself. You realize the ultimate truth that mind itself is empty. Then, it all opens up and you see there is nothing but emptiness. There is not even the tiniest particle that inherently exists. This realization of emptiness is the realization of the nature of the emptiness of the mind, and its functions. These functions, this creating of the reality of the conventional world we are used to is, again, based on fundamental ignorance, which has no realization of the vacuity of all duality. Thoughts and conceptual activity are all dualistic by nature, since their existence comes from our fundamental ignorance of the true nature of reality, including all ordinary thoughts and concepts. These give rise to grasping and clinging, greed, desire, and anger. They are all mental creations. When we practice meditation, cultivating the state of Shamatha, the perfect one-pointed concentration of mind taken to its ultimate degree, all these thoughts, although they do not disappear, they cease to disturb the mind. Then, with insight meditation (Vipassana), we can see through the illusion, and see things as they are. We become like a skillful surfer at the beach. Ordinarily, if you go to the beach not knowing how to surf, when you see the big waves coming at you, while in the water, they seem frightening. They can knock you down, becoming an overwhelming and unpleasant experience. However, if you are a good surfer, then you can dive right in, the waves are no challenge, and you can have fun with them. That is what happens in the practice of meditation. You can observe things; wave after wave of conceptual thoughts, you can go with them without being disturbed, without being carried away by them. All emotions, all sources of desire and misery are passed by without affecting you. You remain in that peaceful place of observing these things without being caught up in them. This develops, increasingly, as you practice Shamatha and Vipassana meditation. You gain more and more of that calm detachment. Finally, you become free of their influence. The two great lessons of the Heart Sutra are that all things are empty, and if we do not understand this, we undergo all of the miseries of the world. It is the mind that is the source of all the bondage of Samsara, with all of its suffering, and, the liberation from it, is the state of complete bliss. This is why the practice of meditation is absolutely necessary. Because things do not exist in the way they appear to exist, we are caught up in ignorance. Ignorance is the confused state of mind whereby it obscures reality from the mind. It is because of this we wander, repeatedly, through Samsara. When we see things and believe them to exist as they appear, we attach ourselves to them. We see something that is beautiful, we choose it, and cling to it. If it is something we do not like, we feel aversion, and move away from it. In this way, we are involved in Samsara; we are involved in this constant suffering. Then, when death comes, not having realized the emptiness of all appearances, we think about the things we will miss after our death: our homes, our friends, our family, this, and that. You take up the aggregates again, picking the things, you desire, and throwing away the things, you do not like. All because you are trapped in this illusion of what appears as existence. On the other hand, if you free yourself from it at the time of death, there is no difficulty: your consciousness leaves, and goes straight to Sukhavati, to the Pureland. That is why it is so necessary to overcome cognitive errors, the fundamental ignorance, and why one must practice meditation. To realize emptiness, you need to meditate. Meditation is part of a threefold process of developing the wisdom that realizes emptiness. The first process is the discriminative awareness that arises from study, and from hearing teachings. The second process is the wisdom of contemplating them, and coming to understand them. The third process is the wisdom arising from meditation. Here, meditation means to accustom the mind to the realizations that come from meditation, getting to the point where it is one's reality. In meditating on emptiness, you look for the nature of reality. First, you want to realize the mind because you know the mind is empty, but you have to perceive the mind, therefore you meditate, and when you meditate, you do not see the mind, you see the proliferation of conceptual activity. Finally, after practicing and developing the skill and concentration, the coarse level of conceptual activity subsides. Your mind becomes peaceful, and, at that point, you can look for the mind, and you will find that it does not truly exist. Then you look for the Buddha. You want to attain Buddhahood. You look and look, you meditate, and finally realizing that Buddhahood is empty. The Buddha does not truly exist. The search for anything that truly exists, of, and by itself, when carried on to completion, comes to the point that nothing truly inherently exists. The

79

realization of the empty nature of inherent existence is the realization of ultimate reality. Developing that further, while in meditation, habituating the mind to see things as they really are: completely free of inherent existence, you eliminate all the subtle propensities and latencies to grasp things as truly existing. This way, you remove all obscurations to attaining the state of perfect enlightenment. By cultivating the transcendent wisdom of the Prajñaparamita in the practice of meditation, you will attain ultimate enlightenment.

Doubts may arise when you say that nothing whatsoever truly exists. You may ask if this it not falling into a nihilistic view. This is a challenge, because there are the views of non-buddhists who do not believe in an ultimate, absolute, truly existent reality, and they would say that it is a nihilistic view. Even among those who cling to the solitary nirvana, some would like to hold that the lack of belief in a truly existent world constitutes nihilism. However, it is not a nihilistic view, because it is not a denial of appearances. It is, instead, an insight into the nature of appearances. It is the non-grasping of appearances, not the denying of appearances. With the realization that all appearances do not truly exist, that they are like a dream, you become free of their influence. Like great waves, all conceptual thoughts, and all phenomenal appearances, can wash over you. You are fearless, because you will never be caught up in them. That is not to say that they do not exist, they appear, but they do not exist as they appear. As a result, you become completely free from their influence, yet you are completely aware of all phenomenal appearances. Your clinging to them has ceased completely. Because you ceased clinging, you no longer have an attachment to desirable things, and an aversion to those that are not. Without attachment and aversion, appearances have no power over you. That is why you attain the state of complete freedom. It is only from this point of view that you can truly practice the Six Paramitas, engaging in transcendent giving, patience, so on, and so forth, which benefit living beings. This is the state of the truly enlightened being: accomplishing activities for the welfare of limitless beings without even trying. That means that a fully enlightened one has no apprehension of truly existent living beings. A fully enlightened one realizes the emptiness of all living beings, as well as everything else, so there is no apprehension of these truly existent beings needing help. There are no truly existent beings. This is the delusion.

The mind of the Buddha compares to a flower. The flower has nectar. The bees and the flies drink from that nectar; the nectar nourishes and sustains them. The flower has no intention to feed insects; instead, it is its nature. Likewise, the sun illuminates the world, but it does so because it is its nature. Likewise, the fully enlightened one, benefits countless living beings because that is the nature of his fully enlightened mind.

Next, the text describes the good qualities of wisdom. What are the good qualities of wisdom that realizes emptiness? The quality is that if one has the wisdom that realizes emptiness, one is free from all fear. The mind becomes completely free of fear. Fear comes from seeing things as being truly existent, and being subject to their power. For example, if you are in a dark place, you think you are alone, and suddenly you see what looks like a person, and you become fearful, then, you find out that what you saw is just a picture. Seeing into to the actual nature of that object of fear, you become free from the fear. Another example is that you are in a dark place, and there is a rope coiled up. It looks like a snake, to the point that it evokes fear in you, but realizing that it is not a snake, but rope, you lose your fear. When you see that all phenomena, without exception, lack true existence, then you are freed from all fear. Being free from fear, you are free from obscurations. The term obscuration means the imprint on the mind that takes place from habitually seeing things as truly existent. Even if through your analytical meditation, you realize things are free of inherent, or true existence, you still go about your ordinary business. Things still appear to be truly existent; and it is because of these latencies, which are obscurations. These obscurations come from habituation. It is through practicing and accustoming the mind to the way things exists, that these obscurations, which are the propensity of the mind to see things inaccurately, will be eliminated. For example, blow on your watch crystal; it will fog up, although it is not part of the crystal. When left alone, it goes away. Therefore, when you are no longer reinforcing dualistic thoughts that hold things to truly exist, then they will go away. It is through emptiness wisdom that you go beyond all of the errors of the ordinary person. That is to say, the errors that led to all misery, the errors that led to constant birth and death. You go far beyond the limited wisdom of the Sravakas that merely overcomes the afflictive mental states that only liberates themselves. You go beyond that, and you go beyond what is called 'the immature views of worldly philosophers', who are so deluded by appearances that they cling to them and make all sorts of silly statements about things they believe to truly exist. Then, if you go beyond even the clear realization of the Pratyeka Buddhas (Solitary Realizers), and their sphere of activity. You cut off, not only the afflictive obscurations, but also the cognitive obscurations, and obtain the state of omniscience. It is through the realization of emptiness that you eliminate the cognitive obscurations, the subtle latencies, and these impressions on the mind. You actually see all things, without exception, as being completely free of inherent existence. You eliminate every type of afflictive mental state without exception. For example, Sravakas and Pratyekabuddhas like to try to eliminate the coarse defilements, and that is like trying to wash the dirt out of your shirt: you keep washing it, trying to get rid of it. The Mahayana practitioner, realizing that eliminating cognitive defilements is like taking the shirt off, and throwing it away: you do not have to worry about washing the dirt out. All of that defines the good qualities of the wisdom that realizes emptiness.

The effect of 'Wisdom Realizing Emptiness' is the attainment of the peerless and supreme state of the manifest Buddhahood, because of all of the Tathagatas of the past, present, and future, abiding in this 'Wisdom Realizing Emptiness' (Prajñaparamita), and thereby they attain that state of perfect and ultimate Buddhahood. The sutra states, again, that all of the Buddhas of the three times abide in the Prajñaparamita, that the Prajñaparamita is the Mother of all the Buddhas.

The Dharani (Mantra) of the Prajñaparamita

The term 'De Tha Be Na', or Tadyatha in Sanskrit, means: 'and therefore'. It is the introductory word of

83

the mantra. It sums up everything stated in the sutra. Everything in the sutra leads to this mantra. Because the mantra of the Prajñaparamita is the mantra of Supreme Awareness, the unequalled mantra, the mantra eliminates every vestige of suffering. It is, in no way, false. Understand it to be the actual truth. These are all the qualities of the mantra. We should understand this, because the mantra contains, within it, the essence of all the Prajñaparamita teachings. If you have the ability to realize it, then you do not need those teachings, you just need the mantra, because the mantra contains the entirety of the Prajñaparamita. It is the heart of the Heart Sutra. It is the mantra of Supreme Awareness. In the text, it says it is the 'equal to the unequalled'. What is the unequalled? The state of supreme enlightenment is the unequalled. It is beyond the state of the ordinary world. Not only that, it is beyond the state of nirvana of the Sravakas and the Pratyekabuddhas. It is beyond everything: it is unequalled. The Prajñaparamita is equal to this unequalled state. It says in the text that this mantra eliminates every vestigial misery. This goes without saying, if you fully realize the Prajñaparamita, you transcend all misery. Merely reading it has great benefits to overcome ordinary suffering such as illness. Just the reading of the sutra has that power. The recitation of the mantra helps overcome the various ills, and they are eliminated. Not only does the recitation of the mantra eliminate the sufferings associated with illness, it also protects against all negative influences, and the harmful actions of humans and non-humans alike. In sum, the recitation of the mantra eliminates all the various problems, troubles, and miseries of the world. You should understand that the mantra is the expression, in syllables, of the Prajñaparamita. The Prajñaparamita eliminates all ignorance. Ignorance is what causes all troubles, all suffering, all misery, and all the difficulties of the world. It is in that sense that through reciting the mantra, one eliminates all ignorance, and through that, one vanquishes all misery without exception. The mantra translates as: "Therefore, through going beyond, completely beyond all illusion (the illusion of inherent existence), one attains Bodhi (the highest enlightenment), 'svaha' means 'and so it is'. It is the ordinary mind, in becoming free of the afflictive states, which becomes the Buddha and attains enlightenment. This mantra contains the essence of the teachings of the Prajñaparamita, and therefore contains all of the powers, and blessings of the fully enlightened Buddha.

Then, in the text, the Lord Buddha arises from His profound samadhi, gives the 'thumbs up' sign, and says: "Way to go!" to Avalokiteshvara. "It is just like you said! In fact, all of the Buddhas of the past explain the Prajñaparamita in this way, in the present, we explain it in this way, and in the future, all Buddhas will explain it just as you have said." We can understand, then, that the view, given in the Heart Sutra, of Vipassana, which analyzes and realizes the nature of reality as emptiness. Vipassana is the meditation that realizes the Prajñaparamita, and the practice of Shamatha makes the practice of Vipassana possible. Shamatha is the focusing meditation. It is the ultimate attainment of the perfectly concentrated mind, in our ordinary state; we are like that person caught in the surf, with the waves pounding over one's head, and the body tossing about. In that state, one cannot focus calmly and clearly. You have to get beyond that. Therefore, Shamatha is the state where the mind becomes so calm and clear that it is unmoved, and untouched by these waves of mental afflictions and conceptual thinking. It is like being in a totally clear and calm pond. It is only from the state of Shamatha that the mind becomes calm and clear enough, so that one can begin to penetrate into the nature of reality. That one can begin to realize what it means for phenomena to lack true existence. Only when you have that clarity, is the mind not under the influence of attachment and aversion, and attains that perfect, effortless, one-pointed focus. The Prajñaparamita is within one's own mind. It is not to found elsewhere. When you allow all these adventitious defilements to subside, then the Prajñaparamita becomes clear. You realize it, and attain enlightenment.

Seven Point Mind Training (Lojong)

Today, we look at Seven Point Mind Training, called 'Lojong' in Tibetan. This is a very important text, because, in the seven points, it sums up the practice of the bodhisattva. The practice of the bodhisattva is the essential practice taught by the Buddha, the Buddhas of the past also taught the same, as will the Buddhas of the future. If we seek to practice Mahayana Buddhism, in its entirety, it is a daunting task. Therefore, in their kindness, the Buddhas and their followers, the great teachers, summed it up in a concise manner. In addition, the Lord Buddha said that if we do not practice everything, even practicing a small part of the Bodhisattva Path has tremendous benefit.

The text opens with homage given to Avalokiteshvara. The text pays homage to Avalokiteshvara, as he is the embodiment of the compassion of all Buddhas. He is said to be the great hero of the Bodhisattvas, as he attained his qualities through the Perfect Peerless Wisdom, and he engages in the activities of pure and limitless compassion. Therefore, all the wisdom and compassion of the Buddhas can be found within this one figure: Avalokiteshvara.

The lineage of this teaching comes, as do all dharma teachings, to us from the Lord Buddha Shakyamuni, from him to his disciples, and down, through generations of masters and disciples, to the present time. This covers many generations. We will not go through that, but rather to point out that it comes from the Buddha down to the great teacher Suvarnadhipa, and from Suvarnadhipa to his disciple, and into Tibet, down to the teachers of the Kadampa, and from there to the present time.

The subject matter of Lojong is bodhicitta, the mind of the bodhisattva. This mind of the bodhisattva is the essence of the mind of the Enlightened One. Therefore, it is what the Buddhas teach. It is compared with two things: one is with the nectar of immortality, and the other is with the diamond. It is said to be like the elixir of immortality, because through the practice of bodhicitta, all Buddhas attain the transcendence of death. They attain this deathless state beyond all birth and death. Therefore, because they attain that with the practice of bodhicitta, Lojong is called 'The Nectar of Immortality', also called 'The Diamond', because it is the most precious practice to be found. The diamond is the hardest known substance, and even a small diamond has great value. A small drop of the 'Nectar of Immortality' has great power. Likewise, even generating a little bit of bodhicitta has tremendous benefits. If you fully generate it, then you become a Buddha, but even a small amount will be of tremendous value. Bodhicitta is like the sun dispelling darkness. When Bodhicitta arises in one's mind, the darkness of ignorance, and the mental afflictions disappear. At this time in the history of the world, this era of decline, or degeneration, is a time where there is an increase in all bad things, and a decrease of all good things. The bad things are those, which harm living beings. There is an increase in the impulse of sentient beings to harm each other. Thinking that harming others, they will gain some benefit. When sentient beings feel harm or threatened, they tend to strike out, and harm someone else. This shows how the times have declined, because through harming others, one only harms one, and does not benefit. Five types of unfortunate things mark this degenerating time. The first is life span. Life span is declining. Then, there is the decline with regard to the time, to beings, and understanding. This means that, overall, ignorance, and all that flows out of ignorance is on the increase. Does everyone have a copy of the **37 Bodhisattva Practices**[28]? The 37 Bodhisattva Practices is a different way to teach Lojong. Take this book, and study it carefully. This little text, together with Seven Point Mind Training, teaches the nature of the bodhisattva mind: how we can practice it, how we can understand it, and incorporate into our daily lives. Here again, in this degenerate age, where problems increase, and in general, solutions become scarcer, it is of vital importance to focus oneself on generating bodhicitta. This is the light in the darkness. This is the cure for the ills of the world. This what transforms all of these problems, and brings about the welfare of all beings, you included.

To follow this teaching on Lojong, and how to cultivate bodhicitta, you must first understand the nature of human existence. To take birth as a human being is very difficult. Among all the different life forms, this is very rare. Being a human being is extremely valuable because it is only in human rebirth that one can practice the Dharma, and receive its benefits. Only as a human being, can we cultivate bodhicitta. To take birth as a human being is very difficult. We have that rebirth now, and we should make the best of it. Most humans, although human, have no ability to practice the Dharma. They have no

---

[28] The 37 Bodhisattva Practices, by Ngulchu Thogme Zangpo. See Appendix for the entire text.

89

access to it, no opportunity to receive teachings, and so forth. We are not like that. We have attained a human body, as well as the 18 types of leisure and opportunity that make it possible for us to practice the Dharma. Therefore, this is a very rare opportunity, and not one to be wasted, because if we lose it, how can we expect to gain it in the future? The eighteen types of leisure and opportunity are what we have when we have full access to the Dharma, and the ability to practice as human beings. The first one is the good fortune. It is the endowment, with certain things, which allow for the practice of Dharma. These right types of leisure are the freedoms that come from not being born in the five other realms of existence, not possessing the wrong views that prevent one from entering into an understanding, not being born in a place or time where a Buddha does not come to teach Dharma, and finally, not being born with impaired faculties. The ten types of opportunity that must exist in this human rebirth, divide into five that are one's attributes, and five that are the attributes of the environment where you live. The five personal attributes are: first, one takes birth as a human; second, that one takes birth in a place where the Dharma exists; third, that one takes birth with unimpaired faculties; fourth, that one is free of the deadly sins, the extreme forms of bad karma; and fifth, that one is in possession of faith in the teachings. If you do not have faith, then having the other attributes is of no avail. You need to have that faith, which connects with the Dharma. Then, there are the five types of opportunity that pertain to the environment. The first is the Buddha has come into that world; second, the Buddha has turned the Wheel of Dharma (taught the Dharma); third, that these teachings still exist; fourth, that there are followers of that teaching (practitioners who are alive); and fifth, that there are those who make possible the practice of Dharma with their help and generosity. If these conditions are not present, one has to fend for oneself it would be impossible. Wherever I go, here and there, people give me food: it is an example of the conditions being in place. I do not have to worry about certain things, and I devote my time and efforts to practice. The first of the 37 Bodhisattva Practices involves the possession of the aspects of leisure and opportunity. Understanding the rarity and precious nature of human rebirth endowed with leisure and opportunity, it is necessary to go to the next step, which is to comprehend that this is not a permanent state of affairs, rather that this human life is unstable and transitory. It is subject to death. We do not know when death will arrive, therefore, understanding the preciousness, and rarity of human rebirth; we should not waste this opportunity. If we waste it, when will it come again? It could be a very, very long time, many rebirths before we become human once more. As this life is so fragile, so easily lost, what happens if we lose this precious human rebirth? If, during this life, we engaged in no particular virtue, made no effort to help others, then it will be very difficult, because, once we die, and lose this body, we have no power over what happens to us, that is to say, over what rebirth we will take. Our karma determines it. We are completely under the power of our karma. Therefore, if we have not engaged in virtue, then there is no way we will get a decent rebirth. On the other hand, if we are someone who liked others, concerned with them, tried to help them, and did things to benefit them, and then we will certainly gain a fortunate rebirth. Therefore, it depends on what you do in the here and now. Do we engage in things to help others? Do we engage in virtue? Even a small amount of virtue has great power to bring about a good rebirth. In the 37 Bodhisattva Practices, if you look at number 10, it tells you what you should think about to generate virtue. There is nothing higher that we can do than to generate Bodhicitta, the altruistic aspiration to help all living beings to attain happiness, and transcend all their miseries. To do that, we start out by understanding that other living beings are related to us. In former lives, they have been our own kind mothers, and it is necessary to return that kindness. The attitude of self-cherishing is the antithesis to Bodhicitta. Self-cherishing is the mind closed in on itself. This is the attitude where we think only of ourselves at all times: how to take care of ourselves, how to gain advantage over others, and, as a result, the concern is directed only inwardly. This causes great isolation from others, and brings nothing but suffering in the end. It is, in fact, because you think so much about how to take care of yourself, how to advance yourself, and it is those thoughts that cause harm to yourself. When, however, you look outward, thinking of benefiting others, it causes and brings about your own benefit. This is the nature of Bodhicitta; it is the mind seeking the ultimate welfare of others. This is the highest benefit you can bring to yourself. In the 10th stanza, you look at others as your own kind mothers of past lives, becoming concerned with them, and while recollecting their kindness, you wish to repay them, this equalizes yourself, and all others. So that you do not fall into the trap of favoritism, toward some, and not to others, as everyone was your own kind mother, treat all equally. This is the beginning stage in the generation of bodhicitta. Going beyond that, you do the exchange of self and others, whereas, instead of self-cherishing, you cherish others.

The practice of the bodhisattva path has its foundation in the realization that one has had innumerable past lifetimes, and that each living being, without exception, has been your own kind mother in the past. Through comprehending the debt of gratitude you owe to each living being, you act accordingly. This is a fundamental aspect of the bodhisattva's activities. If we ask ourselves, "why is it that we wander in Samsara, from beginningless time to the present, undergoing all of its inherent sufferings?" Self-cherishing is the basic cause of all our misery. If you look at the next of the 37 Practices, number 11, it makes the point that all suffering, without exception, comes from our wishing for our own happiness: that is self-cherishing. Where does the perfection of enlightenment come from? It comes from cherishing others, wishing for the benefit of others. This is the principle of the Bodhisattva's fundamental practice of exchanging self and others. The ordinary world attitude, which returns harm for harm, bases itself upon an ignorance of one's relationship with others, and ignorance of the nature of cause and effect. That is to say that, in our innumerable former lifetimes, we have accumulated various karmic debts, when, for example, in a past lifetime, we harmed someone: that is a karmic debt. We have to pay for it, when that karma ripens, like a seed, which waits for the right conditions to sprout. It ripens in the form of something bad happening to oneself. Then, when that harm comes to us, we get angry again, and cause harm, again, to someone, repeating the cycle, causing the suffering to go from great to greater. On the other hand, if we understand that whatever harm comes to us is the result of some fault of our own, in this, or a former lifetime. That this is the payback. We can accept it without anger. Instead of striking back at someone, we can practice forbearance, and not cause harm, and in this way, all of the bad karmas of the past can ripen, and in ripening exhaust themselves, without creating further outcomes.

The term 'Lojong' (transliterated: mental training) means that we train our mind to think in different ways: to go from an ordinary self-cherishing mind to a new way of thinking, which is a mind that cherishes others. In understanding the nature of cause and effect: whatever arises in the world, as experienced, is the result of karma. We can, then, let go of the thought that anything bad is the fault of someone else. We realize that it is our own fault. It is the karmic result of what we have done in the past. It is completely inappropriate to blame others. Whatever bad happens, it is appropriate to blame oneself, and whatever good happens, to be grateful. Looking at one's misery and certainly one has misery because bad things happen, however, if you look at the world, you can see that your misery is but the misery of one person, whereas the misery of others is boundless. How many people suffer so greatly? How many living beings undergo such misery? When you open up to that reality, you look at it, and see how much greater is the misery of others compared to oneself. Then you become concerned, through this mental training, with the relief of other's misery. You take it upon yourself, unconcerned with your own suffering, and seek some way to relieve them of it. In mental training, you cultivate the ability to do that by viewing your own suffering as limited, and that of others to be great. Even when you inhale and exhale, you visualize taking into yourself, with inhaling, the suffering of others, taking it away from them. When we realize our connection with other beings, not only looking at the superficial relationships going on right now, but when we look at and realize our deep and profound connection with every living being, then our concern for them continually increases. All living beings become our family members. Certainly, when one loses a close family member, we have tremendous grief and suffering; and when someone we do not know passes away, we do not have that grief and suffering. It is because the closeness of the one, and the distance of the other, but as we come to the awareness of our deep connection with all other living beings, then our loving concern for all of them, and our wish to help them, increases. Looking at the events of the past several weeks (September 11th, 2001, and its aftermath), and how many were killed in this great tragedy, with developed insight into your connection with all beings, your wish to relieve others of suffering increases greatly. You now have concern for the welfare of, not just a few, but of all: the Bodhisattva's attitude begins to arise. As this concern for others increases, you naturally think about what you can do to help all suffering beings. This feeling gives rise to virtuous activities, which directly help others; but there are so many others, so many who need help, so many who suffer, and in one's present state, one is limited in what one can do. Of course, when a great number of people die, one is very limited in what one can do directly. The practice of Lojong, of developing the Bodhisattva mind, transforms the mind first, and from that transformation, you become concerned to the point of

95

having the profound wish to relieve others of their misery. Once the mind takes on that resolve, that compassionate attitude, then all good things will come from that. Even though you may not have the resources, or ability to help someone far away, you can transform your ordinary mind into a compassionate one, which will, one way or another find a way to help. That is why we think of the All-Compassionate Avalokiteshvara; pray to him to develop this state of mind, and recite the Mani to bring about that direct connection with his mind to cultivate that level of limitless compassion. When thinking about benefiting others, we can accomplish many things to relieve their temporary miseries occurring in this world. As things in this world are temporary and fleeting, we can seek to relieve beings of miseries they confront: like hunger, thirst, and illness. However, as we develop in our practice, we seek go beyond that transitory level of help, and bring about a true transformation, and to do that you have to remove the true causes of suffering. You first have to identify them. This is why the Lord Buddha taught the cause of suffering, which is the afflictive mental states, and principally the Three Poisons of greed, anger, and ignorance. All harm comes from these poisons; therefore, if you are going to relieve sentient beings of suffering, you have to bring about the transformation in their minds, which removes the Three Poisons. This is why the Buddha teaches the Dharma. We have to be very clear about the fact that all suffering comes from these negative or afflictive mental states. For example, when you go from one lifetime to another, and each time you die with strong worldly desires, how will you attain the Pureland? The way to attain the Pureland is by letting go of your worldly desires, and by seeking to be reborn in the optimal state where you can help others. If you have strong worldly desires, you will be reborn in the world. If you have strong anger, it brings about a low rebirth, such as in one of the hell realms. All suffering comes from states of mind. Realize that and remove these causes of suffering from your mind, and help others in their realization. The Three Poisons are the basis for all self-cherishing. What happens when we cherish the self? When we focus on our self, and when anything difficult happens, even the smallest inconvenience, it is blown out of all proportion, dominating one's thoughts and actions. In doing this, even those around us who suffer greatly, do not get our attention because we are so caught up in our own inconveniences and frustrations. This is the result of self-cherishing. The contrast to this is the mind of the Bodhisattva, which cherishes others. When one is so concerned with the welfare of others, then one's own problems fade away because one is no longer interested in them. This is why the Bodhisattva has such great patience. Personal harm does not bother, or shake, the Bodhisattva. The benefit for others, and oneself, arises from an understanding of the causes of suffering. You cannot get rid of them until you understand what they are. There are 84,000 categories of suffering, they are subtle variations of the Three Poisons, but they all boil down to these three basic mental afflictions. Looking at their functions, we see that through anger, and all of the afflictive mental states associated with anger, we act in ways that bring about unwanted results. Specifically, any action motivated by anger brings harm to oneself. Actions motivated by worldly desires, such as grasping and attachment, bring about deprivation in the future.

The third poison is delusion, or ignorance. The results are also bad. You can say all bad things, in way or another, all worldly misery, our wandering in Samsara, is the result of delusion. You can say actions have a basis in fundamental ignorance. How do we become aware of this? Is it sufficient to just change our modes of thought and action? The best thing that can happen is for us to experience suffering. It is because of suffering that we begin to seek its causes, and we come into an awareness of cause and effect. Only when we begin to see that all our misery comes from our afflictive mental states that we can do something about it. What is it that we can do? We can enter into the Bodhisattva Path, and live in the practice of the Six Paramitas: the six types of bodhisattva activity. If we do not suffer any misery, and everything is fine, then we do not think of cause and effect. We do not try to root out the causes of suffering. We do not think of benefiting others. Consequently, misery is a great source of benefit.

Part of the mental transformation of Lojong practice is to change one's attitude about one's own misery, to increase one's concern for others to the point of not noticing our own, and by seeing the virtue of our own misery. The experience of our misery, spurs us to understand its causes. Another way to see the virtue of our suffering is to realize when something happens to us, it is the result of accumulated karma. That, in many former lifetimes, we have accumulated some serious bad karma, they are like loans we take out, and, at some point, and we must repay them. When something bad happens, it is the payback. Through awareness of cause and effect, you become determined not to repeat the causes of your suffering, and not engage in negative activities in the future. When misery does come, as it does even to great practitioners, one accepts it.

The Great Satan: self-cherishing, from self-cherishing comes afflictive states of mind, from these come all karmas, and from that comes wandering and suffering in Samsara. It comes down to self-cherishing. If we get rid of self-cherishing, we produce no more afflictive mental states: we get rid of misery. So long as we have self-cherishing, misery will flow forth. This is the main concern in the Buddha's teaching. There are various strategies: first, we look at how it functions. Self-cherishing is focused on the body, not on the mind. We are always concerned with taking care of the body: feeding it, giving it good things, making it comfortable, and cherishing the body as if it is the self. Of course, this is very foolish. The body is ephemeral. It is changing every moment, and it will be lost soon enough. When death comes, it is lost. It is like a bubble: it cannot stay. The body is subject to so many vulnerabilities; so many things can destroy it. To place any confidence, or real importance, in the body is very foolish. We will lose our bodies, and when we die, we cannot take it with us. The mind goes on to the next life. To cling to, and cherish the body is a great fundamental suffering. On the other hand, when we can let go of the clinging, then we eliminate most of the footing for self-cherishing. This is why there is the practice of making offerings. If you look at some beautiful thing, you cling to its beauty. It is the action of self-cherishing. The appropriation of something for the self, gives rise to a chain of events leading to misery. What should we do? Instead of constantly grasping, the practice of the Bodhisattva is to constantly offer them. Therefore, instead of saying: "I want that", you look at a beautiful thing and say, "Oh, how beautiful", and offer it to the Three Jewels. We make it as a mandala offering. Anything that we have an attachment to becomes a source of misery. Instead of thinking of ownership, worrying about keeping it and protecting it, immediately offer it to the Three Jewels as a mandala offering. In making the mandala offering, you offer all good things. You offer your possessions, whatever you feel some attachment to: make it into an offering, a real offering. Once you have given it to the Three Jewels, do not think of it as your possession: it belongs to the Three Jewels. Do this, not only with small possessions, but with everything that you own, your home, your resources, your wealth, and do it with your body too, remembering that your body is a transitory thing. You cannot take it with you. It is very vulnerable, easily lost, and clinging to it, is just a source of misery. Therefore, you offer the body to the Three Jewels. When you offer everything, you are free. Your mind is at peace, cleansed of worldly attachment, and is no longer vulnerable to the vicissitudes of ordinary life.

The topic of the generation of bodhicitta is the central topic of Lojong and the central topic of Mahayana Buddhism as well. There are two types of bodhicitta, the conventional, and the ultimate. The conventional, we looked at earlier, and this has to do with the active involvement in transforming the mind, according to the laws of cause and effect. The 37 Bodhisattva Practices mention Ultimate, or Absolute Bodhicitta, and though it cannot match point by point with Lojong, there is a lot of overlap. The 22nd practice states that appearances are one's own mind. From the very beginning, the mind's nature comes from extremes of elaboration, meaning the extremes of existence, and non-existence.

They are mental fabrications. They are elaborations and false concepts. The mind's nature is free from that. The mind conceives, as we went over earlier, the world, as we perceive it, the phenomenal universe. The phenomenal universe does not exist of itself. Therefore, it lacks inherent existence, and is like the objects we perceive in a dream. That is the way we should consider it. All phenomena are like objects in a dream. During the sessions on the Prajñaparamita, we examined how all things lack true existence, so that, if we look at the things that compose our reality, and analyze them carefully, we will find nothing there: we will only find mental creations. If we look at our physical bodies, and compare them with bubbles in foam, which are substantial enough to take shape, we find them to not be substantial. It is the form aggregate composing one's physical body. Then you have feelings, another major constituent of what we call a person, and feeling are even less substantial than form. Feelings are quite ephemeral, changing from moment to moment, they are said to be like bubbles in water, which are quite fleeting. If we examine all things, we see that they are just appearances created by the mind. When we focus on the mind, and look at the mind's own nature, we see its tremendous creative ability to produce a world. However, when we look at the mind itself, we get insight into reality. All phenomena are a projection of the mind. The kleshas, the mental afflictions, are the great enemy, and because we do not understand this, we do not take this enemy seriously. Constantly, we go under its influence, lifetime after lifetime. When we start to understand the great power and sinister effect of these mental afflictions, realizing them to be the true enemy, then so-called worldly enemies, such as other people, are trivial, meaningless, and unworthy of identifying them as enemies. The real enemies are the kleshas. When we see that these are the causes of our misery, then we take up arms against these enemies and give it no quarter. The minute any afflictive state arises, we oppose it. For instance, if we see how harmful anger is, then the minute there appears a small tendency towards it in ourselves, we realize the great negative impact of our anger, how it creates worlds of misery, then we stop it. That is the nature of these mental afflictions; if you look at them, they go away. If you stop and say: "Oh that is anger arising", the anger goes away. Associated with mental afflictions, is conceptual activity, called 'vikalpas'. This is what clouds the mind, and just like the clouds in the sky obscuring the sun. When you identify them, you look at them in meditation, and they dissolve. The Lojong text says that the antidote to mental afflictions is 'self-liberated'. It is the universal antidote, because mental afflictions give rise to all karma and misery. Therefore, to get rid of the very root of all sufferings and illusions, you need an antidote, which is the realization of emptiness, and to realize emptiness, then the topic of the other night, the Prajñaparamita, fills the bill. Again, to summarize, the realization of emptiness is to realize that though things exist, they do not exist of and by themselves. The lack of true existence is their emptiness. When you realize that, you have the clarity that realizes emptiness, the antidote said to be self-liberated. It is self-liberated, because clinging to the concept of emptiness, itself, becomes an obstacle. However, in reality, it will not become an obstacle because emptiness itself is empty, and the clear mind, realizing emptiness is not different from emptiness. That is the meaning of the term 'self-liberating antidote'. Subject-object duality is the basis of conceptualization, and mental afflictions. The realization of a lack of inherent existence eliminates it. Therefore, you have the joining of the antidote, the mind realizing emptiness, with emptiness itself. Through the application of the antidote, all misconceptions, which are like clouds in the sky, dissipate. The mind is in its own nature. When you meditate, all troublesome concepts, thoughts, and images disappear like vapor does when the sun comes out. You abide in the nature of the mind. Abiding is the nature of the path: the setting of the mind in its actual state, like the empty sky free of clouds. In the meditative state called 'the meditative stabilization on emptiness', the actualization of that state is to see nothing. If there is anything there that is identifiable, you have not perceived reality. In the meditative state, you realize emptiness: you realize the complete lack of even the tiniest bit of inherently existent phenomena within the mind, or outside it. It is a transcendence of the appearances in the phenomenal world. When you come out of the meditative stabilization, called the 'subsequent attainment stage', in this interval between stabilizations, again, phenomena appear to you. However, having directly perceived the lack of inherent existence, they no longer fool you. They have no power over you. This is called 'seeing all things as if they were an illusion' you see them as if they were objects in a dream. The simile here is that all things are like an illusion: when we die, the 'reality' we have now, ceases to exist. Just like a dream, it no longer has substance. We can also think in terms of everything that happened in the moment before right now, every moment of the past, is like a dream, and is no longer there. All things, without exception, are like the objects and appearances in a dream.

What about all the negative and troubling circumstances that we come upon in the here and now? We can use them as the path to enlightenment. It is clear that we have to take this path, because we have plenty of negative circumstances. It gives us plenty of fuel for the vehicle that leads to enlightenment. We have a great deal of fuel, and should greatly advance. The way is to understand the process of cause and effect: all problems in the animate and inanimate worlds come from misdeeds. Misdeeds come from the mind, and the mind itself creates all this. We need a technique to use all the negativity, the problems, and sufferings. The technique is the realization that one's misery results from one's commission of negative actions in the past. That realization leads to two things: one is the resolution not to commit harmful actions again because of the ensuing results. The other is the paying back of the loan, the settling of karmic debt, and using up one's bad karma. With respect to the miseries of others, understanding, therefore, that suffering is useful, and by experiencing it, one can advance on the path, welcoming the taking upon oneself, the miseries of others, and, in exchange, giving them whatever happiness one has, whatever virtues, and anything that is beneficial. In that way, one uses all negativities, all harm, to advance on the path to enlightenment. There are other ways to meditate on the good qualities of one's own misery. Misery, if helplessly endured, is nothing but misery, and does not have good qualities. When you accept and understand that to attain the state of enlightenment beyond all misery, you have to pay back the loans caused by your past misdeeds. In other words, you have to use up your bad karma, which stands between you, in your present state, you in your fully enlightened state. Understanding misery to be part of this process, which brings you along to enlightenment, then it is gladly accepted, and endured without bitterness. It takes on a profound meaning now, because of causes committed in the past; in using it up, one commits to no longer plant the seeds of such misery, and then one becomes ever closer to the goal of liberation. In the text, it mentions a statement by a Kadampa Geshe by the name of Gar Gon Cham where it says that every bit of misery you have, uses up your store of negative karma, and brings you closer to the goal, and closer to the future experience of true, unsullied enlightenment. Therefore, he says it is good to consider and think about the good qualities of misery. In fact, harmful or negative circumstances are a spiritual teaching. He says: "My spiritual teacher is my negative circumstances, my obstacles and problems are what exhort me to accomplish virtue." We can see how this is, just in the normal course of events; we all lose those who are near and dearest to us. Our loved ones die, and when they do, we plunge into misery. It is that misery and grief that can be our teacher, and cause us to better understand the nature of the world, to engage in virtue. For example, when one near and dear to you dies, then at night you have difficulty sleeping, you wake up and say some Manis, you visualize Avalokiteshvara and accomplish some virtue. If nothing had happened, you would not have accomplished any virtue. In the larger sense, this is true, if our lives are trouble-free, we never think about cause and effect, the pressing need to accomplish virtue and purify our minds. It is only when things go bad that we come to that, so that we are exhorted by bad circumstances and obstacles to practice virtue. A good example is Milarepa, who, in his very early years, was a pampered child of a rich landowner. His father died, his uncle stole the estate, leaving Milarepa and his family in a state of poverty and despair, and it is from that point that Milarepa started on his path to enlightenment. Had everything gone well for him, he would not have been so inclined. In the sutras, the Lord Buddha says that, when we engage in the practice of Dharma, the arising of various miseries is a very good sign of using up bad karma. In general, all obstacles that arise are conditioned by cause and effect, and we know they have no ability to abide in themselves when we understand the Dharma. They have no reality, no substantial existence. If we let them go like clouds in the sky, they would blow away. They have no ability to maintain their troublesome nature, they will pass, and just like clouds pass and the sun shines. So long as we engage in the practice of the Dharma, we will rid ourselves of these things. In the 37 Bodhisattva Practices, number 18 states that, even though you are impoverished, and disparaged by others, afflicted by illness and tormented by evil spirits, if you can abide that discouragement, and take upon yourself that suffering, and all the miseries of others, this is the bodhisattva's practice. Why is it the bodhisattva's practice, because it leads to the highest enlightenment; these bad conditions, bad qualities of life, are seen as something to advance with on the path. It enables one to cultivate patience, the realization of the nature of cause and effect, the realization of emptiness, which come, not from the ephemeral pleasures of existence, but rather from its ephemeral miseries. It is the miseries, which cause us to appreciate the troubles of others, and to develop compassion and insight. For all these reasons, the Seven Point Mind Training text says the 'four unwanted worldly concerns'[29] cause us to attain liberation. Khenchen Kathchug, another teacher in this tradition, elaborates this point in the text. He wrote that if you are happy, if something good happens to you, then dedicate this to the happiness of all. On the other hand, if you are suffering, then use this to understand how bad misery is, and take upon yourself the misery of all others. Seek to relieve all others of their suffering.

The text says, next, that the root of all virtue is bodhicitta, and that the vast virtues of the bodhisattva, come from the practice of the Six Paramitas[30]. From where does the practice of the Six Paramitas, come? It

---

[29] The Four Unwanted Worldly Concerns are loss, pain, disgrace, and blame as opposed to the Four Worldly Concerns, which are gain, pleasure, fame, and praise.

[30] The first principle of enlightened living is the perfection of generosity. This is what is called charity (caritas) in the Christian sense, which means love; it does not just mean giving pennies to the poor. Caritas means unattached generosity, boundless openness, and unconditional love. Open heart, open mind, open hand, that is why it comes first among the six. It is extraordinarily pertinent to our lives and our path. The second is virtue, ethics, and morality. The third is patience, tolerance, forbearance, acceptance, and endurance. This ties into the fourth one: energy, diligence, courage, enthusiasm, and effort. The fifth is meditation, absorption, concentration, and contemplation. The sixth is the enlightened principle of transcendental wisdom.

arises out of the bodhisattva mind: from bodhicitta. If you possess bodhicitta, then when you see anyone in any sort of need, you seek to fill that need. Whatever it is they need, you give it, because you want to help them. That is the 'bodhisattva impulse': to always help others, to always do what benefits others. The perfection of generosity comes from bodhicitta. The perfection of ethics comes from bodhicitta. If you are concerned with the welfare of all beings, looking upon them as you would your children: that is the practice of ethics, not harming others. Likewise, the practice of patience, comes from bodhicitta: this all-loving, all-compassionate concern for the welfare of others, even if they do something harmful to you, you do not mind it, and you do not strike back. You practice patience. All the virtues of the bodhisattva base themselves on a loving and compassionate attitude. Bodhicitta is the source of all virtues. In order to attain Buddhahood, one needs to accumulate a great amount of merit. What does it mean to accumulate merit? It is the accumulation of compassion and loving-kindness. If you have compassion and loving kindness, then whatever you do is meritorious. This is called 'building the accumulation of merit.' In worldly terms, thinking only of this life, this one little, narrow time between birth and death, there is a tendency not to accumulate merit, but material things instead. If you devote your life to that, then when death comes, you cannot take any of that with you, but you will take the accumulated avarice and stinginess. This leads to a lower rebirth. On the other hand, if you accumulate merit by developing loving-kindness, and compassion, then when you die the loving-kindness and compassion go with you. It will take you from this life into a better rebirth. Compassion and loving-kindness are the basis for building up an accumulation of merit, and that merit sees you, not only, to a better rebirth, but it builds up until you attain the state of perfect enlightenment.

Then, we have the Four Preparations (preparatory activities), which lead to the attainment of enlightenment. The first one is the accumulation of merit. When we understand the virtue of the accumulation of merit, when we see the tremendous value of a compassionate, loving mind, then we make an effort to accomplish it, and make efforts to get rid of anything contrary to it. The second activity is the action of eliminating non-virtues. Eliminating non-virtues eliminates their potency. Non-virtues function to cause suffering. They are the basis of all suffering. When we harm another person, we create karmic effects that are huge. The suffering in the next life will be immense, because we are carried away by that negative impulse, and by the karmic effect of whatever harm that we accomplish. Therefore, if you look at those who destroyed World Trade Center, the Pentagon, and the thousands of people a few weeks ago killed and wounded, and those connected with them, suffer greatly. The harmful effects are incalculable, but you could say they will be calculated; there is no karma (action) without a corresponding effect. Therefore, those who engaged in this destruction, thinking themselves to be virtuous, so deeply immersed in ignorance that they acted that way, bring such misery upon themselves is almost incalculable in terms of the great suffering that will come to them in the future. This is true, of course, even in small cases. Misery always comes from non-virtue. The Bodhisattva's practice is to abandon even the slightest harm to another living being. Looking upon an insect with compassion, and abstaining from harming any living being whatsoever because you understand the unpleasant nature of suffering, and the process of cause and effect, you will do everything you can to avoid causing yourself even the smallest misery in the future. The third preparatory activity is the knowing how to deal with demonic forces. This is a concern because there are many, who have trouble with various types of demons, and understand that you give them their power. Like every other phenomena, they lack inherent existence. The solution, as with every other problem, comes from within, and therefore; if there are very greedy demons, then offer them some nice tormas. Demons cannot resist nice tormas. This way, you use your impulse of generosity to deal with demonic problems. Of course, there are those obstacle-making entities that are rather intractable, and you cannot bribe them with tormas. For them you should engage the practice of generating profound loving-kindness. Developing a clear and active sense of loving kindness and compassion, the real desire for welfare and happiness, for these unfortunate obstacle-making demons, turns them around and even changes them into helpers. The fourth preparation is the practice of making offerings to the Dharma protectors. Dharma protectors are those super-human beings that have an affinity with the Dharma, wishing to guard it and its followers. They can be very helpful in removing obstacles. It is very good to help them with their work, and make offerings to them. Honor them and give them tormas. Bodhicitta is the foundation of these four preparatory activities. If you have bodhicitta, even towards those who seek to harm you, you will not have that angry reaction. If you respond in anger, then it damages your Bodhisattva Resolve. The practice of the bodhisattva is to maintain compassionate concern, even in the face of harm. The real harm is the karmic retribution for one's own misdeeds. Do not be angry with another person, and understand that all such karma comes from the afflictive mental states. You should not personalize things, and become angry with another person. Making offerings to demons, or others, stems from compassionate concern. It is to make them happy, and give them something good. Doing this with selfish motivation, the desire to gain an advantage, is just a worldly activity, and will not be a part of the process leading to liberation and enlightenment. The foundation of the Four Preparations must be the compassionate and loving motivation of the Bodhisattva.

We come, now, to the fourth of the seven points of mind training, here the text talks about the teachings of what is to be accomplished in this lifetime. There are ten items, and they divide into the 'five powers of the present life', and the 'five powers at the time of death'. With regard to the 'five powers of the present life', first is the power of benevolence. Whenever you engage in a practice, as mentioned here, for example the recitation of Manis, but actually in any activity, you should do it with the power of benevolence. This is a key point because there are those who make a mistake here: when they do a practice, their main thought is that if they do the recitation of Manis, they believe it will help them, and thereby help them develop some degree of personal attainment. It is inwardly directed, but again, it is only self-cherishing. Dharma practice, if done in this way can even reinforce self-cherishing, therefore you must avoid practicing in this way. Approach any activity with the thought that you are not just doing it for yourself, but rather, you do it explicitly for others. Your mind opens up completely, and you say mantras for all living beings, which automatically includes yourself. This is the benevolent attitude, the power of benevolence. The power of benevolence must inform all your deeds. It must be done with consistency, and constancy. This is the advice given here in the text. When you wake up in the morning, you bring it to mind right away. Say to yourself: "I am practicing Dharma. Practicing Dharma means to benefit others. What can I do today to benefit others?" Your whole orientation, from the time you get up in the morning, until you go to sleep at night, focuses on helping others. You can even make a promise, a commitment to avoid all self-cherishing: "Today, from now until I go to bed tonight, I will avoid all self-cherishing thoughts, and will work to benefit others." Therefore, whatever you do, when you eat, for example, you think how you can act more beneficially to others. Whatever the activity, there is that outward orientation, that impulse to benefit others, and not that selfish grasping, that always looking to get that 'best thing' for yourself. Therefore, when you look at other beings, you look at ways to benefit them. Discriminating between loved ones and strangers is an aspect of self-cherishing. Strangers should also be objects of your benevolence. The power of benevolence should be practiced with equanimity, that to say, with equality towards everyone. Therefore, when you get up every morning, you generate bodhicitta, doing three prostrations to the Three Jewels, and again at night, three more prostrations to the Three Jewels. The second of these five powers for the practice of the Dharma in this life is the 'Power of Familiarity'. It is the familiarizing, or habituating the mind to the practice of bodhicitta. The practice of the bodhisattva is to act in benevolent ways towards others at all times: from the smallest benevolent act, to the greatest one, which is establishing beings in the liberation of Buddhahood. To do this, you have to accustom the mind to the great benevolence of bodhicitta. As you begin to practice this, you can find that sometimes you feel very benevolent, and other times you get angry. Anger harms and destroys the bodhisattva attitude: therefore avoid anger. For example, when you are driving in your car, and someone cuts you off, you get angry, and that anger destroys the effort you have been making. You have to apply an antidote, rather than getting angry, you think how unfortunate what difficulties this person is taking upon himself by having this sort of bad behavior. Instead of anger, you have compassion. This takes habituation. You have to work at it and become more accustomed to behaving in this way. The more accustomed you become, the more natural it is the less frequently you fall into anger. The third power is the 'Power of the White Seed'[31]. This refers to that which gives rise to bodhicitta. Bodhicitta is something, which has to be developed, or cultivated. It has to take birth within the mind. In order cause bodhicitta to develop, and arise within the mind, you need to accumulate merit. Without merit, you will not give rise to bodhicitta, and without bodhicitta, then you look upon others from the perspective of your own self-cherishing. That is to say that even with your mother,

---

[31] 'White' here means stainless, or virtuous.

you might not have any good feelings towards her, and wish for her happiness, thinking instead how she inconvenienced you, or is quarrelsome. Therefore, to generate that profound benevolence, it is necessary to have merit. Otherwise self-cherishing continues, and it becomes stronger. Like this last week when so many people were killed at the World Trade Center, for those who have very strong self-cherishing, they think: "Oh, it would have been horrible if I had been in that building, but since I was not, it was not so horrible." It is not that one would say that, but it is the feeling, someone so focused on him, does not feel the misery of others, and does not concern himself with it. Therefore, not being concerned with it, the actions that follow are those that make such things possible. If you have concern for others, and eliminated self-cherishing to a significant degree, it comes, again, from building up the store of merit. How do you build up merit? The way indicated by the Lord Buddha, is the 'Seven Limb Practice'[32]. When you build merit this way, then benevolence becomes stronger, and comes to the point of generating bodhicitta. Merit accumulates in many different ways, but there is a key element, it is the element of faith. The element of faith, you look at the image of Vajrasattva on the altar, over there, and you have a little bit of faith while looking at it, even if for a moment, great merit comes from that. It could be the image of Avalokiteshvara, or another deity, just that spontaneous feeling of faith from the heart, accumulates tremendous merit. Rinpoche says that he

---

[32] It is paying homage, making offerings, the confession, and purification of sins, rejoicing in the welfare of others, exhorting, supplicating, and dedicating.

carries the image of Avalokiteshvara with him, and every time he looks at it with a little faith, great merit arises. This is true of any object of devotion, or like looking at the teacher who is teaching you some Dharma, and you think how wonderful it is that someone is bring into this world this precious teaching of the Buddha. It could be that you are looking someone counting mantras on their beads, and think how excellent that there are people like this in the world. Each time you have such an experience of faith, each time some object like that arises in your mind, great merit results. Making an offering of a flower you see, and offer it to the Three Jewels with the mind of faith, great merit comes from that. If you take it instead, and decorate yourself with it, that is feeding self-cherishing, it is not great merit; it is the reinforcement of the negative. Merit comes from all offerings, physical or mental, it comes from your heart. What is bodhicitta, this mind of a bodhisattva? Its essence is this kindness towards others: the fully developed mind of kindness. It is not different from any kindness, any compassion that we have. To fully develop bodhicitta means to develop more and more compassion, and a loving attitude towards others. When we see great suffering, and we respond to it with compassionate feelings, this increases the compassionate aspect of our mind. It develops bodhicitta within us. When we look at the tragedy in New York, how many thousands died, and that each person there had a mother and a father, maybe children and a spouse. How greatly each of them suffers, each of them having a network of relations and friends, and the misery of that event involved so many people, each person was like us, each not wanting suffering for themselves or their loved ones, how terribly sad the event is. Then increasing your loving kindness, your compassion for others, bodhicitta develops the way. It is the development of an active sense of loving concern wishing them happiness, seeking to free them from any suffering. Normally, we have the genuine heart-felt, loving attitude and compassion towards those who are dearest and closest to us, but when we look at someone else, someone we have never seen before, we might not have any sentiment or kindness towards them. As we realize, through understanding the cause and effect nature of all things, that that person was, a former lifetime, our own kind mother who bestowed upon us such benevolence, automatically we feel kindness towards him, and have the wish to help him. Even an insect that buzzes around, if we think of it as totally different from ourselves, not having any relation to it, we can chase it and swat it away, but if we realize that insect was actually our mother in a former lifetime, and was so kind and caring, then you will look at it very differently. You will treat it with kindness, and cultivate a loving attitude towards it. We have come to the next section, the fifth power. It is the defining quality of Lojong. What is it that distinguishes Lojong? The answer is that if we look at all the vast teachings of the Buddha, the 84,000 categories of the Dharma, the Lojong is the most essential principle, and it is this internal aspect of all the teachings, that the Buddha conveys, regardless of vehicle or lineage. It is the way we can rid ourselves of self-cherishing and transform our minds. How do we transform the mind? We transform it in order to banish this self-cherishing. For example, if you are practicing mantras, such as Manis, with a self-cherishing attitude by thinking you will profit from it then, this is not

116

Buddhist practice. When you recite mantras, you recite them for helping others. The fundamental nature of your practice must be to help others, and not be self-cherishing. Now we can begin to understand why it is said that the essence of Seven Point Mind Training is the abandonment of self-cherishing. Because this is the essential feature of the Buddha's teaching, then, whatever we do as Buddhists, must be consistent with the elimination of self-cherishing. If it is not, then no matter what the appearance is, it is not Buddhist practice, because it does not lead to the cherishing of others instead of oneself. The text states next, that we can understand this principle as the witness of our practice. The essential feature of Buddhism is the cherishing the welfare of others, and abandoning self-cherishing, then the judge of the validity of one's practice, is that principle. It is not possible to pretend, or act like one practices, but in the mind, cherishing the self. It is in the determination of one's deepest motivation that one asks whether it is to help others, or to help oneself, and in that determination one know that validity of one's practice. This always has the support of a 'Joyful Mind'. 'Joyful Mind' is what occurs when you have you have eliminated self-cherishing. Self-cherishing is the root cause of all unhappiness and suffering. If you banish it, and you have the cherishing of others in mind, then your mind is freed from all the hopes and fears that torment the minds of ordinary beings. In that sense, you have the 'Joyful Mind'. This is the peaceful and joyful state of mind, which can accomplish the benefits of others.

The next statement in the text says that you are proficient if you can practice even when distracted. The example given here is of riding a horse. If you are a skillful rider, then even in rough terrain, you can stay and manage on the horse, and continue on your journey without difficulty. Likewise, if you are skillful in meditation, that is you know how to use mindfulness and vigilance in your practice, keeping the mind focused on its object, then, even in difficult circumstances, you maintain your meditative focus. Difficult circumstances are both the external ones of adverse conditions, and the internal ones, which are the mental afflictions. When they begin to arise, before they can manifest, you cut them off and eliminate them through heedfulness. Nothing will disturb your mind.

Under the commitments of Seven Point Mind Training, you will find the 'Three Principles'. The first is the 'Great Mind'. The second is "Great Upholding of Discipline'. The third is the 'Great Austerity'. The 'Great Mind' is to continually hold as your deepest commitment, should be bodhicitta. The 'Great Upholding of Discipline' is the extremely careful avoidance of even the smallest misdeed. The 'Great Austerity' means that there are many types of austerities. As an example, we can look at Jetsun Milarepa, and how he gave up all worldly comforts, sitting in a cave without clothes to keep him warm in the freezing weather, practicing austerities. What is the 'Great Austerity'? The greatest austerity, in looking at Milarepa, is not the physical one, but it is the internal austerity of conquering the afflictive mental states of anger and delusion.

The 'Great Religious Practice' is never to separate from all of the Dharma activities of the Three Doors of body, speech, and mind. The last of the Five Powers is the 'Great Yoga'. The 'Great Yoga' is continually habituating yourself to the yoga that joins together

118

wisdom and compassion. It is the 'Great Union'. These are the five aspects of greatness of the Bodhisattva's Mind. The body of the bodhisattva does not have to be very big, but the mind does. The mind has to be huge to be able to encompass all living beings.

In Lojong, there are the sixteen aspects of the sacred commitments, or samayas that one takes up. The first of these, is always training oneself in, and holding the vows one has taken as precious treasure. These can be any kind of vow: the Refuge Vow, the layperson's vow, the monastic vow, or the Bodhisattva Vow. You need to strictly observe them. The next aspect is the practice of patience. The practice of patience is not just limited to having patience with other sentient beings, but also to the natural elements in the environment. We should not indiscriminately destroy them for selfish purposes. Patience, again, not just practiced towards family members and friends, but rather with complete impartiality towards all sentient beings. Next, your inner attitude must transform from doing things selfishly, to doing things selflessly. The fourth aspect is to not talk about other's weak points. This is the training to not say things about the weaknesses of others, even at the cost of your life. It is inappropriate to point out others flaws in public, or in internal dialogue to yourself. A quote from the Buddha explains this teaching in the sutra of 'Exhortation to Higher Resolve'. "For those who wish to develop higher qualities, it is very helpful to abide in an isolated place, then you can have thoughts of the faults of other beings". This means that when you live among others, out of habit, we notice their faults, arising in our mind, this can be harmful, therefore, it is better not to judge at all. One does not talk or think about the weaknesses

119

of others. The fifth aspect is to work on the stronger disturbing emotions first. The text talks, here, not only about disturbing emotions, but about any mental afflictions, which ever one has that are the strongest, disturbing the mind the most, one should work on attenuating them first. The sixth aspect is to give up all hope for results. These are the karmic results of virtuous practice. Do not practice Dharma with the eye on the karmic results of praise and gain. The seventh is to give up poisonous food. What does it mean to give up poisonous food? Poisonous food is a metaphor for mental afflictions. The text says here that: "If you have very good food, but it is mixed with poison, it can cause your death". Likewise, if your practice of the Dharma is very strong, but it mixes with mental afflictions, motivations concerned with the Eight Worldly Concerns[33], it cuts off the light of your path to liberation. The eighth says not to rely on consistency. Consistency here means a history of habituation, which is an attachment to appearances. It is better to rid oneself of the discrepancy between the superficiality of appearances and what is going on underneath. It is the development of true discernment. The next aspect mentioned in the text says to not be adverse to 'cutting the marks'. This means to not engage in undisciplined words, actions, and even facial expressions in public. If you have a quarrel with someone, then do not respond in an undisciplined manner expressing your anger, or displeasure. The tenth aspect says: "Do not wait in ambush", meaning that if you have a problem with someone, do not cherish that problem, holding that ill will, waiting for the opportunity to arise for

[33] See endnote number 3.

confrontation or harm. Waiting in ambush is extremely incompatible with the practice of bodhicitta, because you harbor ill will. It is not an impulse, it is premeditated, and the anger is held for a period of time. It is destructive to the practice. The next one, which is the eleventh of the sixteen, says "Do not make things painful'. This is similar to the tenth. It reflects the allowance of someone harboring ill will. This would be like waiting for someone to go down before kicking him. None of these commitments is difficult to understand. Cultivating bodhicitta, looking upon all beings as having been your own kind mother in the past, and that now, you undertake to cherish them. The twelfth is 'Do not put the load of a Dzo[34] on an ox'. A Dzo is very big and powerful compared to an ox. An ox could not possibly carry him. It is wrong to put a Dzo's load on an ox. What this conveys is that you should not overburden others. In other words, do not give yourself the easy tasks and give the hard ones to others. The bodhisattva's practice is to find the most difficult thing and do that. Take the largest burden upon yourself to relieve others of the greatest burden. The next one says, 'Do not aim to win'. Winning here means overcoming others in whatever competition, and wanting to be the winner, the strongest one. The focus is always on some temporary gain: to concern yourself with that is to lose sight of the overall goal. The goal is to attain Buddhahood for the sake of others. Therefore, whatever happens in this life, it is only valuable if it advances one in the attainment of Buddhahood. The fourteenth one is 'Do not struggle to attain the best thing for oneself'. This is to avoid the tendency of long

---

[34] A Dzo is the name for the male Yak.

habituation, from this and past lives. For example, if you have some food on the table, and you spot the best pieces for yourself, the text is saying not to do that or for the larger concept of taking the best things and leaving the inferior ones for others. The next says, 'Do not reduce a god to a demon'. 'God' and 'demon' are metaphors for Dharma and worldly ways. Reducing a god to a demon is like praying to some beneficial, worldly god, making offerings to him, and persuading him to cause harm to someone. You should keep your Dharma practice pure, and not be motivated by mental afflictions to engage in the Dharma. This would be like doing a practice out of a sense of competition, envy, or the like, and you are doing this practice to make yourself look good, or respected. That is reducing a god to a demon, to diminish the Dharma and transform it into a worldly function. The last of these is, 'Do not seek pain as a component of happiness'. Do not find happiness in the pain of others. This can take many forms, there are explicit ones where you would outwardly rejoice, and then there are the internal ones where you cannot keep yourself from being pleased when you see the harm to an opponent. The text expands on the meaning, because this is important: as the bodhisattva works for the benefit of each living being, then it is to the advantage of oneself, as the bodhisattva, because whatever good thing happens to a living being as a result, is a good thing for you. Any bad thing that happens to anyone is a loss to a bodhisattva. Therefore, it is clear that any sort of rejoicing in the harm that befalls someone, is inappropriate. Rinpoche says that he is always struggling with this one in particular. Wherever he goes, people are suffering some kind of loss for his benefit. That is they spend all sorts of money for flowers, candles, and various kinds of efforts to set up a nice throne for him to sit on and giving up their work and wages to make offerings to him. Although it is very nice, he feels bad because they are losing something from this. Next time a simple wooden chair would suffice then, he will feel less guilt. Save the throne and all the beautiful trappings for when His Holiness Chetsang Rinpoche comes.

We have an opportunity for questions now. Someone asked a question about an ordained Sangha member that misbehaves. If an ordained Sangha member commits some violation of his or her vows, if done in front of us, and we see it, there are many types of violations; there are very fine distinctions of proper and improper behavior, even small infringements. To simplify the issue: that the violation is something you witnessed personally, and it is not some small infringement, such as taking out a shotgun and shooting someone, and you witness it. The answer is at the very essence of Lojong teaching. The essence of Lojong teaching is that you do not ever focus on the faults of others under any circumstance, even in extreme cases. You can even say, "This is my mistake, I am seeing things wrong. Others are much better than myself." You always turn back to yourself, the practice of Lojong; again, the essential practice of Buddhism is to purify your own mind. You cannot go around purifying other's minds; they have to do that for themselves. You have to purify your own mind. You must always focus on your own faults, if you look at the faults of other, you will keep seeing more things to judge, and your mind will get darker and darker, and become more non-virtuous. If you look inwardly at your own faults, your mind will become lighter, and cleaner. That is the practice of Lojong.

Question: "Would that extend to an acceptance of the fact that karma, in the sense that this is obviously a very negative action, there will be a very negative result, so why feed into it anyway?"

Answer: "In the case of someone committing a non-virtue, of course we are aware of the law of cause and effect, and that non-virtuous actions have results that are miserable, because of that, if we are practicing Lojong, when we see someone else do something bad, and the appropriate way is to respond with compassion. You cultivate compassion for that person and develop the wish that darkness of ignorance will be removed from that person."

Questions and Answers

Question: "When you do that, you are holding those thoughts, would it be permissible to take the gun away before they shoot someone else?"

Answer: "Yes, if you do something like that, by a concern for the welfare of others that that person might kill as well as the welfare of the killer. Certainly, taking the gun away is very good. You understand that someone being killed is like everything else in the world, without exception, is the result of cause and effect. Though at some point, the person who was killed accumulated the karma to be killed at this time. If they did not have that karma, he would not have been killed." Rinpoche gives the example of himself, how many times he was shot at by the armies coming into

124

Tibet, and he was not killed. He did not have the karma to be killed.

Question: "If a wrathful enlightened being, such as Miyowa, who stomps on enemies and eats them, how is that consistent with the bodhisattva's practice? Or a mortal who strives to be a bodhisattva, copies that activity for the same purpose?"

Answer: "Miyowa is an associate of the Buddha Shakyamuni, possessing the fully enlightened mind and unlimited compassion for living beings. As noted in the empowerment[35], some beings can be taught by gentle, peaceful means. For example, someone is practicing the Dharma, and is doing some small harmful thing, you can go to them and say to them, 'look, you are trying hard to practice Dharma, but you are doing this thing that is harmful to others, do not do this', and you change their behavior. That is good. However, then some find such virtue in harming others. They delight so much in the pain of others, and see it as something good; such persons cannot be trained, or influenced by gentle, compassionate means. Therefore, you need other means, and that is where wrathful Miyowa comes in: to train the very difficult ones by wrathful means. Miyowa, being all-compassionate, and all-wise, he knows the way to do this. He takes the life of an evildoer, for example, he does so through pure compassion, with no anger at all. He has the transcendent ability to destroy the body of the evildoer, while sending the consciousness, which is

---

[35] His Eminence gave the empowerment, two evenings before, for the practice of Miyowa, otherwise known as Achala, the wrathful manifestation of Shakyamuni Buddha.

never destroyed, to the Pureland. In the Pureland, that person will receive training from Amitabha Buddha. As we, ourselves, are training to be bodhisattvas, we have to ask whether we should follow that model, or not. We do to the extent that we can, we do it with complete compassion and without any anger, and it is very good. If we act with anger, we increase the problem. There is an example of this in the Jatakata Tales[36]; in one life, his name was Captain Compassionate. He ran an ocean going merchant vessel. One time he had five hundred merchants on board, taking them on their trading missions. There was one person among them whose name was Minak Dun Tong Chen. He had an evil plot to kill all five hundred merchants. The captain, the bodhisattva, had no means to stop him except to kill him. Out of compassion, he killed the villain, and happily took the bad karma upon himself. He did it for the sake of others. Likewise, if we are in a situation, where we can save a great number of people by killing one out pure compassion, and with no anger, then that would be a way in which we can emulate the bodhisattva's intentions.

Question: Unintelligible.

Answer: "There are some people who misunderstand, or have partial misunderstanding of karma. What they do not understand is that everything in this world is the result of karma. There is nothing whatsoever that is chance or random. Whatever happens, whether good, bad, or neutral, is a karmic result. To isolate one thing and say, that is karma, usually reflects a great misunderstanding. In any case, because something is

---

[36] The Jatakata Tales are stories of the former lives of Shakyamuni Buddha.

karma, it is not a reason to feel compassion. All suffering, without exception is the result of karma. It is precisely with the function of karma that we are concerned. Cultivating compassion towards those suffering from karma is the same as saying cultivating compassion towards those who are suffering. It is redundant to say karma. Of course, all things are karma. Whenever someone has any misery, we generate compassion, and practice Lojong. What you try to do is to take that suffering from them, take it upon yourself, and give to those beings your happiness, your welfare, and your comfort. It does not matter the circumstance. All misery comes from karma. What kind of karma? Karma is based on ignorance, delusion, anger, hatred, and all of these things lead to suffering. Suffering is, by its very nature, the karmic result of mental afflictions. This is even more reason to feel compassion for those who suffer, and seek some way to relieve them from the suffering, either directly, or by helping them to overcome the sources of their misery.

Question: "We are told in the Lojong that we must get rid of all self-cherishing. How is that consistent with these practices of purification, like Vajrasattva for instance, or relying on the Four Powers to remove your own negative karma? Is that not taking care of you, and thereby related to self-cherishing?"

Answer: "No, when we follow the Mahayana Path, the Path of the Bodhisattvas, everything we do becomes motivated by the concern for others. The concern for others means that we have to help them. We have to actively take the burden upon ourselves in helping others. How can we best help others? Is it by remaining a deluded, ordinary being in the world, powerless against one's own karma? On the other hand, is it by obtaining enlightenment, and obtaining the sublime powers of the three bodies of the Buddha? The way you help others is by getting rid of your own defilements, removing from yourself the causes of suffering and defilement and attaining enlightenment. It is only from the enlightened state that you can truly benefit limitless sentient beings. That is why we engage in Vajrasattva practice and the other practices, to remove our defilements. Defilements are those things that limit us, and obstruct us from helping living beings".

Question: "Can Rinpoche speak to the free-floating anger that Americans are experiencing due to current events. How can we overcome this?"

Answer: "The great anger felt by some people, when there is some outrage like this[37], is expressed in various ways. As Buddhist practitioners, what we are concerned with is looking beneath the surface, and realizing that this anger we feel, we have to understand that our anger and hatred is consistent with the anger and the hatred of those who committed these horrible acts. That anger and hatred is not different, because it is in one person versus another person. Whether it is in a human being, an animal, or any other sentient being, anger is anger. Anger harms the person who harbors it, and harms anyone who is exposed to it. The function of anger is to harm. The karmic result is great suffering for the person who expresses it. Understanding these things, we can see that the true enemy is not the body of the person that has anger, it is not even the mind, and it is the anger in the mind. Anger is the true enemy. Therefore, we cultivate compassion as the antidote to our own anger. We know that we are all

---

[37] The events of September 11, 2001

128

connected, and because the nature of our consciousness is the same as all others, the nature of anger is the same. Therefore, when terrible events like that happen, which are based on anger, we should spur ourselves onward to reduce our anger, to meditate on compassion, and if enough people do that, then the level of anger in the world goes down. This changes the minds of the enemies who do these things. With less anger, and less hatred in the world, the less there is for everyone. It is beneficial to oneself; it is beneficial to those people, and beneficial to the world."

Question: "Is Lojong practice, in its entirety, the same as the Sathyagraha practice of Mahatma Gandhi? Are there differences, and what would those differences be?"

Answer: "Yes, if we look at Gandhi, what he did seems very consistent with Lojong practice. We can see in Tibet, big kings like Songsten Gampo, doing the same thing. These are cases of great leaders, who took the principles of Lojong, and applied them on a large scale. There is the example of a Buddhist nun, when the two countries were at war, killing many people on both sides, appealed to both sides to stop fighting. At first, they did not listen to her. Then she said she would sacrifice herself, in a public event, for the sake of bringing peace. She immolated herself, this had such a powerful impact that the two sides stopped fighting and reached an accord. This should be the impact of Buddhism: to always bring peace between people by any compassionate means."

We now come in the text to the guidelines for mental training. The first of these called 'Accomplish yoga in one way'. What is the one way? You have all these different yoga practices, and yoga is term for the essential practices of Buddhism. They can all be summed up in the one unitary principle of thinking and doing what benefits others. The essential state of mind is the one that seeks the benefit of others. The yoga is to make your mind one with the benevolent mind, which seeks the benefit of others. The next one says, 'All corrections are made in one way'. This shows the essential manner in which we deal with adversity. Adversity then, can come upon even those actively and diligently engaged in the practice of Dharma. Various types of problems, and obstacles, whether it is the harm from others, whether it is illness, whether it is things in the environment, any adverse condition, the Lojong practitioner is advised to see them as an opportunity for a great advancement in one's practice. If things are going along easily, the level of the practice does not change. It is when serious obstacles arise that serious progress can happen. Therefore, looking on these issues as opportunity is very valuable. Instead of when these obstacles occur, you are discouraged, and think that your Dharma practice must not be very effective, or even worse, the practice of the Dharma must not be very effective, you abandon your practice, and turn your back on the welfare of sentient beings. As problems come, you are happy to be taking on these problems: "May they all come to me. May I carry the burdens and miseries of others"; when you feel that inspiration to help others, then you are using the problems as a way to go to a higher level of practice. The occurrence of problems in one's practice specific to the practice for instance, which arise to make some aspect of your practice impossible, then you understand this to be an opportunity, and you make a

130

profound aspiration at that point. "May I, in the future, be completely free of such obstacles, and accomplish this practice without any hindrance". The next one is 'At the beginning and the end of two things to be done'. 'Beginning and the end' means beginning and the end of the day. When you get up in the morning, there should be the firm resolve to spend the day accomplishing the Dharma. You resolve, when you get up, to be free of anger, free of any harmful words, or activities: to be free of self-cherishing. At the end of the day, you can evaluate, and examine what you did. Did anger arise? Did greed arise? Did you do something that was harmful to others? Then can you rejoice in anything good you did, and in any misdeeds, you avoided. With regard to anything negative you did, you should generate strong regret and remorse, resolve not to do it again, and do purification prayers to reinforce the aspiration. The next statement says, 'Whichever of the two occurs, be patient'. The 'two things' are good things and bad things, happy things and sad things; you should practice patience with either. When something good happens, do not let that distract you from your practice. Do not be self-congratulating and carried away by your good fortune. Likewise, when something bad happens, do not be carried away with that. Be patient, understand its nature and karmic result, and keep the mind on an even keel. Focus on your practice. Focus on your bodhisattva resolve as the way to purify your mind, and avoiding non-virtue. The next item, the fifth one, says 'Observe these two, even at the risk of your life'. The two things are the sacred general commitment (samaya) to the Dharma, and the particular commitment to Lojong practice. These must be upheld, even at the cost of your life, because the life

131

will be lost in any case, but do not lose these two things. This is what will sustain you from life to life. Do not give it up, even to save this ephemeral and destructible body. The general commitment to the Dharma is to avoid non-virtue, and practice virtue. The particular commitment to Lojong is the engagement to the cherishing of others rather than self-cherishing. The sixth says: 'Learn the three difficult points'. What are the 'three difficult points'? The first difficult point is the when mental afflictions arise; it is difficult to recognize them. Mental afflictions can be very insidious, and appear in different forms, making it difficult to identify them. You must train yourself to recognize them immediately when they arise. The second difficulty is that mental afflictions are difficult to overcome. You must train yourself in how to overcome them. The third difficulty is that it is hard to sever their continuance, because one affliction leads to another, when one arises, it produces another one. Train yourself in severing the continuum of these afflicting mental states. The seventh statement is: 'Take up the Three Primary Resources'. These are the three causes of the successful practice of the Dharma. You should take these up. The first one is the coming together with a spiritual teacher. Second is the resource of being inspired to accomplish the Dharma. That is the mental resource. Without this aspiration, you will not accomplish it and do what it takes to keep your clearly and strongly inspired. The third is in order to accomplish the Dharma you must have the ordinary requisite of life, such as food and clothing, to sustain you as you engage in the practice. Next, is: 'Do not allow the three things to weaken'. What are these three things? The first is the devotion and respect to the spiritual teacher. What impairs this to weaken and decline is too much focus, other than his teaching. It is a decline of your faith and devotion on the superficial qualities of the spiritual teacher. Is he handsome? Is there something wrong with this teacher? Is there anything wrong about him? It is very good to take teachings from many teachers, and focus on the teachings. Do not focus on the person: focus on the teaching. As was said before, do not look for faults in others. Even if some faults jump out at you, you should identify them as your own misperception and refocus on the teaching. That way the faith and devotion to the teacher is maintained. The second is the taking pleasure in Lojong. It is through seeing the virtues and benefits of the practice that we aspire to Lojong that we take pleasure in doing it. We do not allow it to become something oppressive by seeing it as a duty. Third is to not allow your heedfulness in the practice of the precepts to decline. The precepts of the training require heedfulness. It means you have to cultivate the states of mindfulness and vigilance. You have to observe your mind, because it is the internal practice that is the most important. The ninth commitment is: 'Make the three inseparable'. The three things are the practices of body, speech, and mind. Inseparable means, inseparable from your daily life. You should never be separated from the virtuous practices of body, speech, and mind. You should not just take them up from time to time, but maintain continuity by always engaging in virtues. Virtues of body are things like prostrations, circumambulations, turning a prayer wheel, counting on beads, and all sorts of virtuous activities of mind done with bodhisattva motivation. Virtues of speech are things like recitations of mantras, and the chanting of texts, and so forth. The virtues of mind are things such as the continual contemplation of the faults of cyclic existence; that is to say, the things that give rise to a mind of renunciation. This very important, because if you think of it only on occasion, you will never leave it, understanding that you cannot avoid suffering so long as you are born again and again in Samsara. The only true and meaningful happiness is found in transcending the samsaric state. The tenth statement is: 'Train in all realms without partiality'. This is to avoid chauvinism, or partiality to this world, or human beings, as examples. You should never isolate one small fraction of living beings, but practice Lojong regarding all living beings in all worlds without discrimination. Be all encompassing in the scope of your practice. The eleventh statement is: 'Overall deep and pervasive proficiencies of importance'. It means to be comprehensive in your practice. You do not just do physical activities of Dharma practice, or verbal ones, and mental ones, but you integrate all three. You should integrate, into a comprehensive whole, the practices of body, speech, and mind, not excluding any part. In this way, the practice becomes comprehensive and effective. The next statement says: 'Always meditate on volatile points'. When bad things happen to you, such as a person causing harm, there is the tendency to focus on that person as the problem, then, anger arises. The anger is misdirected, because it is not that person's body, or mind, it is the kleshas, the mental affliction in that person's mind, which arises by the force of ignorance. Thinking that person is harming you, you think you should get angry. By getting angry, you are doing the same thing as they are. You accumulate the causes of your own suffering. The essential point is to meditate on the great harm of mental afflictions. Even if that person steals everything you own, even if they harm your body, you keep your mind on the key point, which is the perniciousness of anger. Whatever happens, you do not allow anger to arise. Anger is the true enemy. On a large scale, where you have one leader of a nation, or a group, causing terrible harm, there is a tendency to focus all the blame on that one person is very great, because if all the blame is there, then you can easily get rid of your problem: you can destroy that person and the problem is solved. This is a great illusion. This is focusing inappropriately on what you think is the key point. That person is just a human being. That person has the same buddha-nature, the same essential ability to become a Buddha as you do. The problem is in the ignorance and anger generated. You should not identify one thing as bad, others as good, and discriminate in that way, but correctly focus on the harmfulness of mental afflictions. It is the same with strong desire, you look at a person or a thing as so desirable, it is all mental projection, instead of anger, and it is desire. This type of discrimination is a mistake, it is ignorance created by the mind. Even with food: some food is laid out, but there is only one item you like, and you neglect the rest. This type of discrimination, of something good or bad, is from an ignorant point of view, from self-cherishing. The idea is to focus on the fundamental problem of greed, anger, and ignorance. The next one, 'do not depend on external conditions', here, you should not make the mistake of thinking that in order to practice Dharma, all things have to be just right. What is the most essential aspect of the practice, is taking on the miseries of the world, and giving it happiness. Having difficulties and obstacles is all the better. It is the ideal time to practice, especially if you maintain the continuity and strength of your practice, even in the face of difficult conditions. The next statement is: 'practice the important points'. This, the fourteenth statement means to keep your perspective on your practice. As there are many aspects to the practice, the details should not distract you. There are two aspects, the explanation, and the accomplishment. You need to have an explanation of the practice to be able to accomplish anything with it. The focus should always be on the accomplishment. A little explanation can take much effort and time to achieve. Always focus on the accomplishment, rather than acquiring large amounts of knowledge that will not be accomplished. What is accomplished? It is bodhicitta. Bodhicitta is the internal accomplishment, the transformation of the ordinary mind into that of the bodhisattva mind, and by doing this, all other aspects of the Dharma fall into place. This is like going some place and looking for something valuable. If you see, in the midst of other things, a precious jewel, do not distract yourself by picking up the other miscellaneous items.

The fifteenth statement says: 'do not make mistakes'. 'Mistake' is a weak word for this, it really means doing things opposite to the proper way. These mistakes are doing things opposite to the proper way they should be done, in six different ways. The first one regards patience, or forbearance. What is the mistake that can happen with forbearance, with being patient in a perverse way? To not have patience with the difficulties that arise in the practice of the Dharma, but having patience with the difficulties in the accomplishment

136

worldly things, especially sinful activities, is like not willing to undergo the hardships of practice. This applies in the internal sense as well, such as not having the patience to train yourself in discipline, ethics, and concentration, but having patience with your mental afflictions, allowing them to arise. The next item is called 'perverse interest'. Instead of being interested in that which appertains to the Dharma, the continual source of all benefit, you are interested in the senseless and harmful activities of the world. It is paying attention to things in the wrong way. Next, is 'the perverse taste' that is taste in the sense of experiencing the taste, or the flavor of things. Perverse taste would like taking pleasure in the experience of things like alcoholic beverages, drugs, and associated objects of sensual desire, and not have a taste for the experience of the sublime Dharma. It is something to abandon. 'Perverse compassion' is next, and this is having compassion for those who are undergoing the apparent difficulties in practicing the Dharma, rather than having compassion for those behaving in harmful, or sinful ways. If you look at the life story of Milarepa, you see that there are worldly people who came to see him in his cave and would think it awful that this poor person, Milarepa, is wasting his life, doing nothing, not eating good food. That is perverse compassion. The next one is 'perverse mental focus'. This would be focusing on the accomplishment of worldly aims for oneself, one's friends, or family. Whoever engages in this, like selling, making profits in business, stealing, or whatever the worldly activity is, at best squanders this lifetime and this opportunity, creating bad karma for countless lifetimes. Next is 'perverse rejoicing'. Proper rejoicing is to rejoice in the virtues, happiness, welfare, and comfort of others, those who rejoice in the hurt and suffering of others, have perverse rejoicing. This brings us to the sixteenth, which is 'do not fluctuate'. It means not to be intermittent in your practice. Your practice should be consistent and uninterrupted like the flow of a river. You will then accomplish the goal. Next is 'train wholeheartedly' with the mind focused on the one central point of bodhicitta, then all one's actions will flow out of bodhicitta, and all will benefit others and lead to the highest enlightenment. The eighteenth is 'find freedom through examination and investigation'. As we are speaking of Buddhist practice, it is internal practice, when you engage in this analysis and examination, it is of your mind, you are not looking elsewhere. This is both in generating wisdom and in generating compassion; you always focus inwardly on the mind. In generating wisdom, your focus is on the nature of the mind, and in generating compassion; your focus is on bodhicitta. Are you developing it? Is it the authentic bodhicitta by having the authentic, true motivation to help others in all your activities and thoughts? The next statement in the text says 'do not make a fuss'. Do not make a big deal of little things you do for others, when you do that it reflects the external, worldly activity of an individual who is looking for worldly gain, not the internal practice of the Buddhist. Number twenty, says 'do not get caught up in irritation'. If you feel frustrated or irritated with someone, there is a trend to have some sort of continuity: they did something to you yesterday, they did the same thing the day before, something that irritated or frustrated you, and you hold on to it. Your irritation and anger accumulates, and at some point, you will do something either you will regret, externally, or giving rise to strong anger. What this means is do not hold on to things. Let go of them, if you continually let go, they will not accumulate, and there will not be bad consequences as a result. The next one says, 'do not be temperamental'. It means not to be too sensitive or moody. The example, here, is of a very sensitive scale, which can tell the slightest difference in weight: do not be like that. Do not be so sensitive to what is going on around you. Be open-minded, and slow to be disturbed. The last one in this list is 'do not expect thanks'. This regards Dharma practice. You should not expect any return for your efforts to help others. You should always do the dharma of helping others from the internal perspective of helping others, not to get some gain or thanks in return. The practice of Dharma is an internal one, a quiet one, it is even said to be a secret one. Doing Dharma practice for the benefit of others is its own reward. The conclusion repeats the great benefits arising from the practice of Lojong. Through this practice you relieve others of their misery, and destroy the basis of you own misery, self-cherishing, and from this, all benefit, including yourself. The text that Rinpoche has been using is the work of his own teacher, the great Gelugpa Geshe Nawang Puntsok.

The Thirty-Seven Bodhisattva Practices By Ngulchu Thogme Zangpo

Homage to Lokeshvaraya!

At all times I prostrate with respectful three doors to the supreme guru and the protector Chenrezig, who through realizing that all phenomena neither come nor go, make single-minded effort for the sake of migrators.

The perfect Buddhas, source of benefit and happiness, arise from accomplishing the sublime Dharma, and as that (accomplishment) depends on knowing the (Dharma) practices, I will explain the bodhisattva's practices.

1. At this when the difficult-to-gain ship of leisure and fortune has been obtained, ceaselessly hearing, pondering day and night in order to liberate oneself and others from the ocean of cyclic existence is the bodhisattva's practice.

2. (The mind of) attachment to loved ones wavers like water. (The mind of) hatred of enemies burns like fire. (The mind of) ignorance, which forgets what to adopt and what to discard is greatly obscured. Abandoning one's fatherland is the bodhisattva's practice.

3. When harmful places are abandoned, disturbing emotions gradually diminish. Without distraction, virtuous endeavors naturally increase. Being clear-minded, definite understanding of the Dharma arises. Resorting to secluded places is the bodhisattva's practice.

4. Long-associated companions will part from each other. Wealth and possessions obtained with effort will be left behind. Consciousness, the guest, will cast aside the guesthouse of the body. Letting go of this life is the bodhisattva's practice

5. When (evil companions) are associated with, the three poisons increase, the activities of listening, pondering, and meditation decline, and love and compassion are extinguished. Abandoning evil companions is the bodhisattva's practice.

6. When (sublime spiritual friends) are relied upon, one's faults exhausted and one's qualities increase like the waxing moon. Holding sublime spiritual friends even dearer than one's own body is the bodhisattva's practice.

7. What worldly god, himself also bound in the prison of cyclic existence, is able to protect others? Therefore, when refuge is sought, taking refuge in the undeceiving triple gem is the bodhisattva's practice.

8. The Subduer said that all the unbearable suffering of the three lower realms is the fruition of wrongdoing. Therefore, never

committing negative deeds, even at the peril to one's life, is the bodhisattva's practice.

9. The pleasure of the triple world, like a dewdrop on the tip of a blade of grass, is imperiled in a single moment. Striving for the supreme state of never-changing liberation is the bodhisattva's practice.

10. When mothers who have been kind to one since beginningless time are suffering, what is the use of one's own happiness? Therefore, generating the mind of enlightenment in order to liberate limitless sentient beings is the bodhisattva's practice.

11. All suffering without exception comes from wishing for one's own happiness. The perfect Buddhas arise from the altruistic mind. Therefore, completely exchanging one's own happiness for the suffering of others is the bodhisattva's practice.

12. Even if others, influenced by great desire, steal all of one's wealth, or have it stolen, dedicating to them one's body, possessions, and virtues (accumulated) in the three times is the bodhisattva's practice.

13. Even if others cut off one's head when one is utterly blameless, taking upon oneself all their negative deeds by the power of compassion is the bodhisattva's practice.

14. Even if someone broadcasts throughout the billion worlds all sorts of offensive remarks about one, speaking in turn of that person's qualities with a loving mind is the bodhisattva's practice.

15. Even if, in the midst of a public gathering, someone exposes faults and speaks ill of one, humbly paying homage to that person, perceiving him as a spiritual friend, is the bodhisattva's practice.

16. Even if someone for whom one has cared as lovingly as his own child regards one as an enemy, to cherish that person as dearly as a mother does an ailing child is the bodhisattva's practice.

17. Even if, influenced by pride, an equal or inferior person treats one with contempt, respectfully placing him just as a guru at the crown of one's head is the bodhisattva's practice.

18. Though one may have an impoverished life, always be disparaged by others, afflicted by dangerous illness and evil spirits, to be without discouragement and to take upon oneself all the misdeeds and suffering of beings is the bodhisattva's practice.

19. Though one may be famous and revered by many people or gain wealth like that Vaishravana, having realized that worldly fortune is without essence, to be unconceited is the bodhisattva's practice.

20. If outer foes are destroyed while not subduing the enemy of one's own hatred, enemies will only increase. Therefore, subduing one's own mind with the army of love and compassion is the bodhisattva's practice.

21. However much sense pleasures, like salt water are enjoyed, craving still increases.

Immediately abandoning whatever things give rise to clinging and attachment is the bodhisattva's practice.

22. Appearances are one's own mind. From the beginning, mind's nature is free from the extremes of elaboration. Knowing this, not to engage the mind in subject-object duality is the bodhisattva's practice.

23. When encountering pleasing objects, though they appear beautiful like a rainbow in summertime, not to regard them as real and to abandon clinging attachment is the bodhisattva's practice.

24. Diverse sufferings are like the death of a child in a dream. By apprehending illusory appearances as real, one becomes weary. Therefore, when encountering disagreeable circumstances, viewing them as illusory is the bodhisattva's practice.

25. If it is necessary to give away even one's body while aspiring to enlightenment, what need is there to mention external objects? Therefore, practicing generosity without hope of reciprocating or (positive) karmic results is the bodhisattva's practice.

26. If, lacking ethical conduct, one fails to achieve one's purpose, the wish to accomplish other's purpose is laughable. Therefore, guarding ethics devoid of aspirations for worldly existence is the bodhisattva's practice.

27. To bodhisattvas who desire the pleasures of virtue, all those who do harm are like a precious treasure. Therefore cultivating

patience devoid of hostility is the bodhisattva's practice.

28. Even hearers and solitary realizers, who accomplish only their own welfare, strive as if putting out a fire on their heads. Seeing this, taking up diligent effort – the source of good qualities – for the sake of all beings is the bodhisattva's practice.

29. Having understood that disturbing emotions are destroyed by insight possessed with tranquil abiding, to cultivate meditative concentration which perfectly transcends the four formless (absorptions) is the bodhisattva's practice.

30. If one lacks wisdom, it is impossible to attain perfect enlightenment through the (other) five perfections. Thus cultivating skillful means with the wisdom that does not discriminate among the three spheres is the bodhisattva's practice.

31. If, having (merely) the appearance of a practitioner, one does not investigate one's own mistakes; it is possible to act contrary to the Dharma. Therefore, constantly examining one's own errors and abandoning them is the bodhisattva's practice.

32. If, influenced by disturbing emotions, one points out another bodhisattva's faults, one diminishes oneself. Therefore, not speaking out about the faults of those who have entered the Great Vehicle is the bodhisattva's practice.

33. Because the influence of gain and respect causes quarreling and the decline of the

activities of listening, pondering, and meditation, to abandon attachment to the household of friends, relations, and benefactors is the bodhisattva's practice.

34. Because harsh words disturb other's minds and cause the bodhisattva's conduct to deteriorate, abandoning harsh speech that is unpleasant to others is the bodhisattva's practice.

35. When disturbing emotions are habituated, it is difficult to overcome them with antidotes. By arming oneself with the antidotal weapon of mindfulness, to destroy disturbing emotions such as desire the moment they first arise is the bodhisattva's practice.

36. In brief, whatever conduct one engages in, one should ask, "What is the state of my mind?" Accomplishing others' purpose through constantly maintaining mindfulness and awareness is the bodhisattva's practice.

37. In order to clear away the suffering of limitless beings, through the wisdom (realizing) the purity of the three spheres, to dedicate the virtue attained by making such effort for enlightenment is the bodhisattva's practice.

Following the speech of the Sublime Ones on the meaning of the sutras, tantras, and their commentaries, I have written the *Thirty-Seven Bodhisattva Practices* for those who wish to train on the bodhisattva's path.

Due to my inferior intellect and poor learning, this is not poetry, which will please scholars, yet as I have relied upon the sutras and the speech of the Sublime

Ones, I think the bodhisattva practices are not mistaken.

However, because it is difficult for one of inferior intellect like myself to fathom the depth of the deeds of bodhisattvas, I beseech the Sublime Ones to forbear my such as contradictions and incoherent (reasoning).

By the virtue arising from this may all migrators become, through excellent conventional and ultimate bodhicitta, like the protector Chenrezig who does not abide in the extremes of existence or peace.

This was written for the benefit of himself and others by the monk Thogme, an exponent of scripture and reasoning, in a cave in Ngulchu Rinchen.

'Drop of Ambrosia'

A Short Practice Of Medicine Buddha

Oral Instructions and Commentary
By Drikung Ontul Rinpoche

Translated by Robert Clarke
Transcribed and edited by Jeffery A. Beach

Introduction

Ontul Rinpoche was born in 1950 in Kham Nangchen, Eastern Tibet. His family lineage, called *Gope* or *Pebon Thogtrul*, originated in pre-Buddhist Tibet. It is one of the thirteen noble family lineages, which stem from the inner lineage of Lodan Nyingpo, one of the four ancient tulkus of the Bön religion. In 1954, His Holiness Drikung Kyabgön Chetsang Rinpoche and his Holiness the Gyalwa Karmapa recognized him as the reincarnation of Ontul Rinpoche, and gave him the name of Tenzin Thrinley Rabgye Palzangpo. Accordingly, he was enthroned that same year at Dong Med Ogmin Thubten Shedrup Ling monastery.

Lama Kalsang Namgyal, the attendant for Ontul Rinpoche's previous incarnation, took the responsibility for his basic education. In 1959, along with other monks and local followers, they fled Tibet together, when the Chinese military occupation began. They were constantly threatened with capture by Communist Chinese soldiers, and suffered from terrible thirst and hunger during their flight. In spite of these difficulties, they managed to cross the border and enter India through Nepal. As there was no place for them to settle, they were forced to wander from place to place for almost fourteen years.

Ontul Rinpoche spent several years in Ladakh, and traveled extensively with H.E. Choje Togden Rinpoche to the many Drikung monasteries there. After coming back to India in 1971, he purchased a piece of land at

Tso Pema (Rewalsar H.P.) with the donations he received from his many different followers. *Tso Pema* means "Lotus Lake." It is one of the sacred places where Guru Padmasambhava demonstrate miraculous powers to subdue the king and people of the region, then known as Sabor. With the help of his monks and followers, he managed to construct a monastery and, over many years, gathered sacred objects, ritual instruments, and other necessary articles. Now the monastery is almost complete. About 30 monks reside there, maintaining the tradition of the Drikung Kagyü.

While in India, Ontul Rinpoche met again with Drikung Khadro Neni Rinpoche, a highly realized yogini, who introduced him to Khenpo Thubten, a great Nyingmapa teacher. Rinpoche received teachings and empowerments from Khenpo Thubten on several important texts, but first was an extensive instruction on the Longchen Nyingthig Ngöndro practice.

On different occasions, Rinpoche received Mahamudra and Dzögchen teachings from H.H. Dudjom Rinpoche, H.E. Khunu Lama Tenzin Gyaltsen, H.H. Dilgo Khyentse Rinpoche, H.E. Kalu Rinpoche, Polu Khenpo Dorje (Sakyapa Khenchen) and others. From the yogi Khyung Ka Rinpoche, he received teachings and personal instruction on the Fivefold Path of Mahamudra. In the following years, he went to Ladakh where he received most of the important empowerments, instructions and oral transmissions of the Drikung Kagyü from H.E. Chöje Togden Rinpoche. Finally, he was fortunate to receive the Six Yogas of Naropa and other important empowerments, teachings and transmissions from the enlightened master Pachung Rinpoche in Tibet.

His previous incarnations are connected with Drikung Orgyen Nuden Dorje, a great *terton* (discoverer of hidden treasures) from the 1800's. Orgyen Nuden Dorje was well known as an emanation of Nyang Ban Tingdzin Zangpo, a great master from the time of King Thri-song Detsen (8th Century). The elder brother of Nuden Dorje was Kunzang Drodul. Kunzang Drodul was born into a noble family lineage in the village of Zalmo Gang in Kham province. The 5th Drikung Kyabgön Chetsang Rinpoche Thugje Nyima (1828-1881) recognized him to be the emanation of Brog Ban Khiu Chung Lotsawa, one of the 25 main disciples of Guru Padmasambhava. Since Kunzang Drodul was the elder brother of Orgyen Nuden Dorje, his successive incarnations are known as *Ontul*, meaning "incarnation of the elder brother."[38]

---

[38] *For further information about Ontul Rinpoche and Tso Pema monastery, please visit their web sites at* http://www.drikung.org

Commentary

Please generate the altruistic attitude necessary to attain perfect Buddhahood. Realize that only through attaining that state of the highest wisdom and compassion will one be able to establish each and every living being who has been one's own kind mother in countless lifetimes in the past. To establish each and every one of them in the true and unchanging happiness that comes only with the attainment of Supreme Liberation. Resolve to listen attentively, to the teachings, to commit them to mind, and then to put them into actual practice. Today we are going to look at the practice of the Medicine Buddha, as contained in this short volume: 'The Drop of Ambrosia.'[39]

The first two lines of the text refer to the refuge, the taking of refuge. The objects of the refuge, that is those in which we take refuge are the Buddha, His teachings, which are the Dharma, and His enlightened followers who are the Sangha. The translation of the first line here, part of it has been left out. What was left out is the term 'tag-tu', which means continually, perpetually. This means that when one takes refuge it is not just for the moment, but it is from this moment on, until one has attained complete, perfect Buddhahood. Up until that moment, one will continue to take refuge.

How will one take refuge? One will take refuge by way of the three doors. One takes refuge physically, verbally, and mentally. Those are the three doors. What

---

[39] The text is titled "The Meditation and Mantra Recitation of the Medicine Buddha called the 'Drop of Ambrosia'". Available through Vajra Publications, Tibetan Meditation Center, Frederick Maryland

is one taking refuge from? One is taking refuge from all of the aspects of what is called samsara, all of the miseries of samsara, all of the dangers of samsara, and so forth. It is from that; one takes refuge in the Buddha, Dharma, and Sangha. One way in which one can think about this, or some people think about this, is that they are taking refuge for themselves and from the terrors of the three lower realms. This means that through taking refuge, they seek to avoid rebirth in the lower realms and attain rebirth in the one of the three upper or more 'pleasant' realms. Another way that some people can think about refuge, when they go for refuge, is to take refuge with the idea of being thereby protected from, not only the miseries of the three lower realms, but from the miseries of samsara in general. Such people take refuge with the idea of attaining the peaceful liberation for themselves. This consists in the attainment of nirvana as an Arhat. This is the case of someone is thinking to attain liberation, only for him or herself. This is the way many people approach the taking of refuge. However, on this occasion, we can see in the following lines, the refuge is being taken, not just to free oneself from the miseries and unfortunate qualities of Samsara. Rather, the motivation for the refuge here is to attain the highest state of unsurpassed enlightenment to free all other sentient beings from the miseries of samsara. This is what distinguishes the Mahayana refuge from other motivations. Whichever of these three types of motivation one has for taking refuge, they are all Buddhist practices because one is taking refuge in the Buddha, Dharma, and Sangha. Therefore, it is said that taking refuge is the very foundation of all Buddhism. It is the first step in all Buddhist practice.

As it is beginning of all Buddhist practice, the Refuge Vow is the foundation of all other vows. As it is the entranceway into Buddhist practice, it is the foundation of all attainments, all of the progress upon the path that is subsequently made. Therefore, if one takes refuge in the Buddha, Dharma, and Sangha, one qualifies himself/herself to be considered a Buddhist.

In this particular line of refuge in the text, it says here "I take refuge respectfully through my three doors"; the term respectful is not quite strong enough for what is being said here. The term in Tibetan is 'gu'i-pay' means devotion. Therefore, it is not enough to be respectful because respectfulness does not necessarily entail faith and without faith, there is no entering into the State of Refuge. The text, indicates in Tibetan the taking of refuge with devotion, with a sense of deep faith in the three objects of refuge and in their ability to provide refuge from all of the miseries and fears of samsara. Refuge is the foundation of all Buddhist practice; it is the doorway, or entranceway into Buddhist practice. Faith and devotion are the foundations of Refuge, the entranceways to taking Refuge. The mind of faith and devotion is so fundamental to attaining the State of Refuge, it is important to look at what is meant here by 'faith and devotion'. There are different types of faith; one is called the 'Faith of Clarity' the completely clear, pure, unobstructed faith arising when one's mind is overcome with devotion to an object. When one just thinking, or seeing, about that object completely captivating the mind. Then the mind becomes completely clear and free of anything else other than that one-pointed devotion, that complete admiration for the object. That is what is meant here. One needs that type of faith; it is the looking upon the Three

Jewels (Buddha, Dharma, and Sangha) and being overcome with this complete sense of devotion.

The second type of faith implied in this statement is called the 'Faith of Desire'. The faith of desire is that aspect of devotion, which arises in respect to an object, which one deeply admires and wishes to attain the qualities of that object. Looking upon the Buddha and being overcome with the magnificence of his attainment, or looking upon the Medicine Buddha and understanding his magnificent qualities of healing and so forth, there arises a desire to attain those qualities. At least there is the aspiration to attain the benefits of those qualities, such as the blessings of the Buddha, the blessings of the Medicine Buddha to overcome all obstacles. There is the desire for what the object of devotion has to give. That is the other type of devotion, which is implied here in this statement of taking of refuge with devotion.

The third type of devotion or faith evoked here is the 'Faith of Confidence'. It is when one's attitude towards the object of faith is free of all doubt, free from all hesitation. One is completely confident of the qualities of the object, believes in them totally without reservation. Of these, three types of faith, the most significant here is the third: the 'Faith of Confidence'. If one possesses this third type of faith, the absolute, unreserved confidence without any doubt or hesitation in the object of refuge, then all of the empowering blessings of the Buddha will be very easily received. One will be able to receive them all. Therefore, it is said, that if you divide the level of your faith into different degrees: lesser faith, middle level of faith, and greater faith, then, relating to that particular type, one will attain three different degrees of blessings: a little blessing, a middling amount of blessing, or a full measure of blessing. This also means if one has no faith whatsoever, one will receive no blessings. This is a very clear exchange of value: if one has faith, one receives blessing; if one has no faith, one receives no blessings. The more faith you have, the more blessings you will receive. The connection between faith and blessing is something of which we should be very aware. What this means in practice is if one has faith in the Dharma, one will get the blessings of the Dharma. Why is that? It is because if one has faith in the Dharma, one will practice it. If one has no faith, if one's mind fills with hesitation, doubt, and lack of clarity, then one's attitude towards practice will be very, very weak. If one has this very clear 'Faith of Confidence', without any doubt or hesitation, then one will undertake, of course, one's practice with enthusiasm. Therefore, the blessings of the practice will quickly accrue. Otherwise, one will be obstructed by one's doubts, one's interest in undertaking practice will be much diminished, and the blessings of the practice will not arise. This attitude of confidence is something we can as powerful in all situations. It does not have to be just in respect to the Dharma. For any effective or meaningful interaction to take place between people normally there has to be some level of confidence. The effective interaction one has with others is based upon confidence. If it is a friend, a business associate, a relative, or anyone like that, in order to work functionally with them in such a way that is beneficial to both people, you have to have some level of confidence. If you have confidence in someone, the more confidence you have, the more efficiently you can work with him or her, the more benefit will arise from that. Understanding that if one is to be effective, even in worldly terms, one will have to inspire confidence in others. One will have to be somewhat trusted by others or else one will not be able to interact effectively with them. Understanding that, one naturally and seriously takes on the task of inspiring others with confidence. Acting in such a way that will lead others to have confidence. Part of the reason this sense of confidence is so important is that it leads to a sense of happiness, or comfort, between people. If you feel confident or trusting towards another, and they feel that towards you, then there naturally rises comfort, happiness, and enjoyment with each other. Interpersonal relationships are based much on trust and confidence in one another. Likewise, when this confidence is lost, when begins to feel hesitation or doubt about someone, one starts to question what that person will do, then tension, uncomfortable feelings, and strife arise. So much of the problem of interpersonal relationships begins in the lack of confidence that people have not succeeded in inspiring and maintaining confidence in one another. On this occasion, we are looking at the Three Jewels as the objects of our confidence. If we are to take up the practice of the Dharma and interact effectively with Buddha, Dharma and, Sangha we must have this confidence in them. It is out of this confidence that we find the faith, that we engage in the practice, and receive the blessings. It is very important to take this seriously, to develop 'Faith of Confidence'. If one lacks it, if one has doubts, then this will undercut or subvert the processes of the Dharma. Therefore, the very first line of the text invokes the Buddha, the Dharma, and the Sangha as the refuge; and follows it with the exhortation to go for refuge in the Triple Gem. One can only proceed through the practice effectively if one truly develops deep, clear, and confident faith.

The next line speaks of other living beings and refers to them as living beings who have been one's own mother, and now tormented and oppressed by misery. The word translated in the text here as 'sentient beings', (in Tibetan 'dro-wa', this is the substantive form of the verb 'to go'), literally means 'goers': those who go, those who move about, animate beings. Called this for various reasons, but principally because sentient beings go from one birth to another. They are called goers because they wander about. They migrate. So, the question is why do they migrate? Why do they wander around? Why go from one realm to another? The answer is they go in that way, because the force of Karma is driving them there. Helplessly driven, they go without plan. They are not deciding: "I will be born in this realm and next time in another realm." They are helplessly driven to take rebirth by their own Karma. There is no laying this out, there is no planning, as if we set ourselves an agenda or a calendar and make plans for what we are going to do in a few weeks or months. There is no ability to do that. Once one is caught in the process of samsara, the cycle of birth and death, one is born repeatedly by the force of Karma. Determination of rebirth, whether it is good or bad, is by one's Karma. The karma, the effect of the activities that drives us, causes us to wander about in a somewhat unconscious, helpless fashion. One's wandering through the various realms of samsara can be compared to an insect, such as an ant, trapped inside a jar. The ant will just wander about crawling up the side, staying a while in one part, then on to another part, sometimes on the bottom of the jar, sometimes wandering up to the top without any sensible plan or strategy. There is no place to go, the lid is sealed tight, and the ant cannot emerge from the jar. Trapped, it can only wander up and down here and there. This is very much the situation for the 'goers', the living beings. This term 'goer' or sentient being refers to all living beings without exception who are trapped in the cycles of birth and death. The text here, "Dug-Ngel Narway", means tormented by miseries. Why are all living beings trapped in samsara? Why are they tormented by sufferings? Why are they tormented by miseries? The reason is that this is the very nature of existence within samsara. It is characterized by misery, so no matter where you go in samsara the basic nature of the experience will be unsatisfactory. There is more and less misery, but misery pervades every single place. It is just like the ant: wherever it goes, it is still trapped in that jar. There is no place in samsara, which is free of suffering. Therefore, it is said that living beings are oppressed by miseries. Understanding this, we have the following line: "La-Me Go-Phang Gö-Chyir Sem-Kye-Do", which offers the solution for all those living beings. The solution is to free them of the trap in which they found themselves. Just like letting the ant out of the jar. It is put in the form of a pledge or a resolve, if you will, showing a determination that we cultivate as practitioners to establish these living beings in the state of ultimate perfect and continual happiness: supreme enlightenment. The verb in the sentence is 'Kye', which means to generate, to give rise to. This is a pledge to generate within one's mind the firm resolution to complete the task of establishing all sentient beings in the Supreme State of Liberation. The object of one's concern, those who one wishes to

162

establish in this state of highest liberation, are these 'wanderers', these 'goers' who are trapped in samsara like the ant in the jar. The text here says: "...sentient beings who have been my mothers.", what does that mean 'mothers'? What this means is that we are trapped in samsara, in the cycle of birth and death. Though it is very large and contains all the different worlds, it is like that jar in which the ant is trapped. It is sealed. We wander around within it. Therefore, in one lifetime, just as in this present lifetime, we have a mother and a father. Therefore, we did in the last lifetime and in the one before that. There is no beginning to the process of birth and death. There is no limit to it. The process is cyclical. It has been going on and on from beginningless time. Each time we are reborn, we have a mother and a father. Therefore, within this closed system of samsara, there is not a single living being that has not been our own kind mother, at one point or another. When we look upon sentient beings, it is not as though we look upon strangers. Other than not recollecting when they were our mothers, it is certain that at some point in the past they were. This entails an obligation to look out for their welfare. It is all the more reason why we should be concerned with freeing them from their miseries and establishes them in the state of highest liberation. This foundation for practice, established through refuge and the generation of altruistic aspiration to attain the highest liberation for all living beings, we now proceed to the actual practice of the Medicine Buddha.

We begin our hearing and contemplation of this teaching by resolving to listen to and practice the Dharma and thereby enable ourselves to establish all sentient beings in the state of Liberation and Highest Enlightenment.

We began this morning by looking at the text 'The Drop of Ambrosia', and went through the first part, which is the taking of refuge and the generation of the Bodhisattva attitude. Now we will continue with some commentary on the meaning of the text and the strategies for practice. The text starts out with the visualization of the Medicine Buddha who we see in front of us. He is seated upon a throne supported by lions. Upon the throne are a lotus, a solar disk, and a lunar disk. Upon that lunar disk sits the Buddha who is the color of Lapis Lazuli. He is the Buddha of Medicine. He is holding a stem of the king of medicinal herbs, the Mairobalan[40] plant, in his right hand. In His left hand, He holds an alms bowl, which again is made of Lapis Lazuli. He radiates the light of the 32 major and the 80 minor marks of the fully enlightened being. He appears in the in the Nirmanakaya form, meaning he appears as did the Lord Buddha in this world, dressed in the three types of monastic robes. We visualize Him surrounded by all the lineage Lamas, Yidams, the seven Medicine Buddhas and Buddhas and Bodhisattvas as numerous as dust particles in the sunlight. The text says 'dust particles in the sunlight' because when the sun shines through a window you can see little particles of dust. Therefore, if you can imagine all of light rays in all directions, there would be innumerable visible dust particles. This to show how extensive the numbers of fully enlightened beings, Buddhas and Bodhisattvas, which surround the Medicine Buddha.

---

[40] Spelling unsure. JB

From the three places, that is the 'Om' in His crown chakra, the 'Ah' in His throat chakra, the 'Hum' in His Heart chakra, go forth rays of light. These rays of light go forth in all directions, taking the form of invitations to the wisdom beings that correspond with each of those being visualized. Those actual wisdom beings are actual Lamas, Yidams, Buddhas, and Bodhisattvas now coming from wherever they are and dissolve into the visualized forms that correspond with them. They are what are called 'the pledge-beings'. That is to say, those who arise through one's own visualization, and become identical with the 'wisdom-beings', the actual beings that correspond to the visualized beings. So, the Medicine Buddha we visualize in front of us becomes identical with the actual Medicine Buddha; likewise for all of the Lamas, Yidams, Buddhas, and Bodhisattvas. We now have in front of us all of these innumerable Buddhas and Bodhisattvas surrounding the Medicine Buddha himself. All of them take on the nature of ultimate wisdom, universal compassion and the powers and abilities of the fully enlightened being and put them into action to overcome the miseries, which cause trouble for all living beings. They take on their true nature to relieve these miseries and in particular those sufferings arising from illness. As we visualize the deities in front of us, we then make offerings.

The way offerings are made is to generate from our meditation the seven types of offering goddesses, each specializing in a different type of offering. Each type of the goddesses goes forth making offerings to each of the innumerable assembled enlightened beings, principal among them the Medicine Buddha himself.

165

Here in the text it says:

'**Sarwa Tathagata**' that means 'All Enlightened Beings';

'**Sapariwara**' means 'together with their retinue'

'**Argham**' means 'the offering water used for drinking'

'**Prastitsa**' means 'please enjoy'

'**Swaha**' seals the offering.

Then you substitute each of the other offerings instead of 'Argham'.

'**Padyam**' means the water for washing.

'**Pushpam**' means flowers.

'**Dhupam**' means incense.

'**Alokam**' means the lamps.

'**Ghande**' means the perfumed oils.

'**Newite**' means the food offering.

'**Shapta**' means the music offering.

Each of these is offered by the class of offering goddesses associated with the particular offering to each and every one of the assembled deities.

Having made the offerings, the next section concerns the offering of praise. It is where the special characteristics that make the Medicine Buddha worthy of our praise and worship are enumerated in brief. The first of these is that His compassion extends to all living beings with complete impartiality. This first defining characteristic of the Buddha is called 'Chom Den Dey' in Tibetan, and in Sanskrit, it is Bhagavan. It has three syllables 'Chom' 'Den' 'Dey'. The first means to overcome, or vanquish the maras. Den means to possess, to possess all the merit, all the good qualities arising from the two accumulations of merit and wisdom. Dey means transcend. What is transcended?

166

The Buddha transcends both samsara as well as nirvana. He does not abide in either of them. He attained the ultimate state of transcendence. He is therefore the Chom Den Dey, the Bhagavan who is equal in His loving-kindness and compassion to every sentient being. The next line says that merely by hearing His name, all of the miseries that living beings encounter in the lower realms are dispelled, this to show His supreme power in clearing away suffering. The next line says, "Divine Medicine Buddha, you clear away the illnesses arising from the three poisons (greed, anger and ignorance)." The three basic types of disease are the processes of wind, bile, and phlegm. They are associated respectively with the three poisons of desire, hatred, and delusion. Clearing away the three poisons one puts in balance all of the bodily constituents and becomes free of disease. Therefore, the Medicine Buddha clears away all of the diseases associated with these three poisons. The last line says, "I praise and prostrate to you Light of the Lapis Lazuli." This part of the practice involves the accumulation of merit through the seven limbs of practice. The first of these is obeisance. This is where we bow down and pray. For prostrations to produce merit it has to be done in a certain way, whether it is done with body, speech, and mind, it has to be done with the mind of devotion and reverence. Obeisance must be performed with deep faith and veneration. It has to be done in a meditative state allowing one to prostrate while offering obeisance and praise to each of the visualized, invoked, and named Buddhas and wisdom beings. To make this offering of praise and obeisance, one has to develop meditative power. To understand what this means, look at the words of this prayer. It defines the way one prostrates says that all of these Buddhas are visualized in front of you. They are as numerous as the little particles of dust that appear in the sunlight. In other words, there are innumerable Buddhas. Meditate on this: upon each particle of dust, there abides as many Buddhas as there particles of dust. Their vast retinues of enlightened disciples surround each of the Buddhas who exist on each particle of dust. In this way, the entirety of space, in all directions, is completely filled with these dust particles. It is to them that we offer praise and obeisance. To be effective, we must do this through the power of our meditation, and emanate sufficient numbers of our bodies to bow down to every one the Buddhas and their retinues. Each of those bodies goes forth with a mind of reverence and deep faith and prostrates to the Buddhas and their retinues. This is something we have to practice: increasing our ability to do so effectively.

The second is offerings, and is what we have covered so far. Third is confession. The third way engages in the limb of bowing to the enlightened beings with one's mind stabilized by 'correct understanding.' 'Correct Understanding' is the understanding that does not objectify the Three Spheres (the Three Spheres being the object to which we bow down, the one who bows down, and the bowing itself). If we objectify any of the Three Spheres, we lose correct understanding. Free the mind that clings to inherent existence of the Three Spheres, effectively we bow down with Right (Correct) Understanding.

The next limb of practice is the Confession. It says in the text: "I confess the evil deeds I committed since beginningless time." This means not only from this lifetime, but also from innumerable lifetimes where there is a tremendous accumulation of various types of non-virtuous karma. This can be purified only through the process of confession, which relies on the Four Powers. Otherwise, one cannot get rid of the effects of the bad karma, and will have to experience the result as great misery or suffering. Principal here are the powers that arise from shame and fear. Shame refers to what one feels when one becomes aware of the presence of the enlightened being. In this case, the Medicine Buddha, the omniscient fully enlightened being from whose wisdom eye nothing is hidden. One realizes then, that the Medicine Buddha knows and understands clearly, all of one's misdeeds from beginningless time to this lifetime. So, one feels a sense of shame. Here, one relies on the first of the Four Powers: the Power of Support. The support upon which one depends for the confession and purification of non-virtue is the Medicine Buddha Himself. Feeling shame when one realizes that He understands all of one's misdeeds. Then, one relies upon Him, confessing to Him, openly expressing one's misdeeds from beginningless time, seeking to hide nothing. One seeks to set things right with respect to Him. He is the support.

Next is the fear that arises when one understands the inexorable nature of Karma. Engaging in an activity, whether good or bad, one will inevitably experience the result, unless one somehow purifies it. The metaphor here is that although one has eaten poison, and has great fear of the sickness and pain will ensue, one will immediately do something about it. This is called the Power of Regret, the second of the Four powers. Here one strongly regrets the non-virtue the one engaged in,

169

because one understands it is poisonous, pernicious nature that can lead to tremendous suffering.

The third power is the Power of Resolve. It is where one understands the consequences of misdeeds, and resolves never to engage in such activities again.

The fourth of the Four Powers is the Power of the Antidote. That is the doing of something that will counteract the effects of the unwholesome activities, such as the practice of Vajrasattva Purification. This is where one meditates upon Vajrasattva and invokes the Purifying Blessings of Vajrasattva. It is seen as nectar flowing out of Him into oneself, clearing out all bad Karma and obscurations; purifying one's body, speech, and mind in that way replacing those unwholesome things with the pure nectar of awareness. Practicing the Vajrasattva mantra, and meditating on the process of purification, this acts as an antidote to the non-virtues. In this way, the Four Powers are put into practice to purify all of one's bad karma.

The next of the seven limbs of practice is the remembrance of engagement in this to build up merit. To have tremendous merit built up through the bowing down, praising and offering to these innumerable beings; the offering to even one of them produces tremendous merit. When one is multiplying one's body to do this produces enormous merit. Then getting rid of all demerits is another aspect of building up merit, because the demerit counteracts the merit, so we have to get rid of that through confession.

Next is the Limb of Rejoicing in the virtues of others. It is the opposite of envy and jealousy. It is where, instead of feeling uncomfortable or unhappy, in seeing the pleasures of others, one rejoices in these things. It is the opposite of envy or jealousy. Understanding that the attainments, the possessions, the pleasures, the good qualities of others, and so forth, arise from their accomplishment of virtue: their generosity and so forth. One rejoices when one sees someone who is happy, someone who good possessions and so forth. Even more, one rejoices in the good, the meritorious accomplishments of others, because this is the highest good that one can do for oneself. To produce merit in ordinary terms, the best action in the world is to do that; and then when one sees someone else do it, one should rejoice in that, without any envy or jealousy. Therefore, the Buddha says that if you, upon seeing the enjoyment and meritorious virtuous deed of someone else, rejoice from the bottom of your heart, then the merit you produce in that rejoicing is equal to merit produced by the person who actually engaged in that virtuous deed.

The branch of requesting the Buddha to turn the Wheel of the Dharma is very important, and again, produces great merit because the Buddha cannot turn the Wheel of the Dharma unless requested. This is why when the Lord Buddha manifested perfect, complete enlightenment in Bodhgaya; there was a period of forty-nine days when he didn't say anything. He didn't teach. His teaching awaited the request for the teaching. The god Brahma accompanied by the god Indra requested it. They came to him, exhorted, and supplicated Him to turn the Wheel of Dharma. Only when requested by living beings in a certain world is it beneficial for the Wheel of Dharma to be turned. Aware of this, we should exhort the Buddha who appears before us to please turn the Wheel of Dharma of the three vehicles (Hinayana, Mahayana, and Vajrayana).

The next branch, which is the sixth of seven, is the entreaty to the Buddhas to stay in the world for the benefit of sentient beings. Fully Enlightened Ones have the ability to withdraw their manifestation in the world and enter into a nirvanic state, but do not do so out of concern for the living beings of the world. However, this can only happen when they are requested to teach. If there is no request, there is no one listening. Likewise, there is no use staying in a place where no one expresses the desire for an Enlightened One to remain. It is very important, then, to request that the teacher remain in the world. This is exemplified in the life of Sakyamuni Buddha, who, many times as the years passed on, remained in the world when requested, instead of leaving. For instance, there was a time when he was ready to go and a disciple named Tsunda begged Him to stay in the world and continue to teach. It was upon that the Buddha remained in the world for some further years. Therefore, the sixth limb is the request to the teacher not to leave the world, but stay as long as sentient beings wander in Samsara. This section of the text ends with the sixth limb of the practice, namely the request for the Buddha to remain in the world for the benefit of sentient beings, as long as they wander in Samsara.

The seventh limb, which is not in the text at this point, but at the end of it, is the dedication of merit of these six limbs. The limbs of prostrations, offerings, confessions, rejoicing in the good qualities of others, the exhortation to teach, and the prayer to remain in the world, are dedicated for the purpose of attaining complete enlightenment encompassing the welfare of all sentient beings. The purpose of the dedication is to protect the merit of the six branches. One has generated all this merit but if one does nothing to protect it, then it will be wasted and squandered in worldly activities. Therefore, instead of letting that happen, one dedicates it to the highest goal. In that way, it is not only protected, it is saved from being squandered on worldly aims. This way the merit will accumulate like a savings account until one attains perfect enlightenment. That concludes the seven limbs of practice.

Please listen to the teachings with a clear and sincere motivation to gradually learn what is being taught. Learn it thoroughly. Put it into practice, progressing from one stage to the next, gradually increasing your clarity and strength of practice to attain the highest state of enlightenment. With the motivation of relieving all living beings of their miseries, liberate them from their cycle of existence and place them in the highest, purest state of happiness and peace, which is enlightenment.

We continue now, as we did yesterday, with the explanation of the practice of the Medicine Buddha called 'The Drop of Ambrosia.' What we've covered so far are the first several pages of the text. First was the process of taking refuge. Next, we have the generating of altruistic motivation of attaining Buddhahood for the sake of others. Then we covered the methods of generating merit consisting of the seven branches of practice. Those three things have now been completed.

If you look on page 6 of the text, having completed the refuge, the bodhicitta generation, and the seven branches of practice, which generate merit. Now, what do with this state of refuge, this bodhisattva attitude we've generated and with all of the merit from the seven branches of practice? What we do is go into the

173

central practice of the Medicine Buddha. Here it refers first to the Medicine Buddha himself. It calls him the 'Bhagavan', 'Chom Den Dey' in Tibetan. As was explained yesterday, the three words (in Tibetan), the first 'Chom' means the He has vanquished all of the Maras and demons. Inner, outer and so forth... 'Den', that He possesses all the good qualities, and 'Dey', that He transcends all limitations of Samsara and Nirvana. That is His nature; He is the fully enlightened Buddha. In particular, as Medicine Buddha, He is known as the 'King of Medicine'. We are addressing Him as the teacher, the Lama, the Bhagavan, the king of all healers and physicians. The second line 'that He possesses in his very nature the great glory of the spontaneous attainment of the two benefits', so spontaneous means that this is His very nature: the attainment of the two benefits. This not something that He has to struggle for or work hard for, but it arises out of His nature. Therefore, He is said to have the tremendous, marvelous glory of this spontaneous achievement of the two benefits. The two benefits are the benefit for oneself and the benefit for others. The benefit for oneself is the attainment of the of the 'truth body', the Dharmakaya. The benefit for others is the attainment of the 'form body', the Rupakaya. The highest benefit that any individual can achieve is the Dharmakaya for him. Then, for the benefit of others they manifest the 'form bodies', such as the Nirmanakaya and the Samboghakaya. These two things are achieved by the very nature of the Medicine Buddha. The next line refers to sentient beings being the object of compassion. They are defined here as all living beings within the realms of birth and death.

What defines them and how we understand their nature, is that they are oppressed by the illnesses of the three poisons. They are tormented by sicknesses of the three poisons. The three poisons are greed, anger, and ignorance. These poisons are the basis of all suffering in the world. Therefore, they are said to be the three *root* diseases, which oppress sentient beings. The next line, in regard to these sentient beings, states that we now resolve to aspire, to engage in activities, which bring about the great happiness and bliss that consists of complete freedom from all these basic illnesses that arise from the three poisons. What we are clearing away with the practice, are the diseases of sentient beings. Therefore, it is important to understand these in order to treat them and bring about the freedom from disease and illness.

The basic roots of all illness as defined here are the three poisons, which disturb, in one way or another, the constituent elements of the body and mind. The poisons, again, are greed (or lust), anger (or hatred), and ignorance (or delusion). These disturb the psychophysical organism. In particular, they disturb the three basic processes, which govern the organism, and those are known as 'lung-tri-began' in Tibetan, which can be loosely translated as 'wind, bile, and phlegm'. The balance of the three basic processes is upset through the influence of desire, hatred, and ignorance. Ultimately, to bring the body into balance and to get rid of disease, we have to deal with these underlying factors. Understanding then, that the three poisons are basis for the disturbance of constituent elements of the organism resulting in diseases, it is also important to understand what is the basis for these three poisons: why do these arise? It is because they have a root cause, what can be called a fundamental ignorance with regard to the nature of all phenomena. Although all phenomena, without exception, lack any self, they lack any 'true' or inherent existence as such. Even though they lack inherent existence, it is through this contamination of erroneous mental process, that one begins to grasp 'self'. This means that one sees things, as being inherently existent, where, in reality, they aren't. For example, with regard to yourself, you see a 'self' that truly exists. This is an example of the contamination of the intellectual conception of inherent existence, and that is what is meant by the term 'fundamental ignorance'. It is from this fundamental ignorance that the three poisons arise, resulting in the various types of unwholesome mental factors. On the physical level, they result in the imbalance of the corporal system, which leads to various disease processes. This type of ignorance, this seeing of things as inherently existing, is called 'innate ignorance' because it is something that comes with us from beginningless time, throughout all of the lifetimes into which we are born again and again. It is not something we came up with at some point. It has always been there. It is the ignorance that falsely construes phenomena to inherently exist. Because of this innate ignorance, the resultant types of imbalances are always with us.

They don't always manifest, even though we are never separated from them. When we are in a state of equanimity, when we are completely free of ignorance, we think we have gained some freedom from the three poisons in the disease process. This is like the bird whose shadow is there but cannot be seen because it is cloudy outside. It just awaits the coming together of conditions, the conditions that allow it to become manifest, such as sunlight. The causal factors are always present for the imbalances of the diseases. They only await the conditions to make them manifest, when those conditions manifest, then suddenly one has one or another type of imbalance or illness. [41]

This simile of the birds helps us to illustrate this, but it only goes so far, because the bird, so long as he is flying under the sun, there will always have a shadow. However there is a way that we can become separated from basic causes of illness, when we become free of their ultimate underlying cause; innate ignorance. Once we've done that, we lack the cause of illness or any type of imbalance. No matter what conditions arise, we will not be subjected to illness. As long as the bird is there, you have a shadow. If you remove the bird, you'll have no shadow. With the removal of 'innate ignorance', there can be no cause allowing illnesses to arise. What we have here is a progression from the ultimate root cause (innate ignorance) to the generation of the unwholesome mental factors of greed, hatred, and delusion and from that to the imbalances of the winds, bile, and phlegm. In this way, we can understand how the processes proceed according to the combinations of the underlying mental factors. We've talked, here, about the specific way in which diseases arise. That is to say, the ultimate source of illness is 'innate ignorance' and the unwholesome mental factors that

---

[41] The tape from the recording had to be turned over, and part of the translation was lost. I paraphrased the intent. It is why I made this section into a separate paragraph. I apologize if this paragraph seems unclear. JB

arise from that disturb the constituent elements of the body, leading to disease processes.

In particular, how do we understand this? What is the precise basis of the arising of each type of illness? Here we have the analysis of the origins, or the etiology, of different types of diseases, and though there innumerable diseases, they can be summed up into three categories. Those diseases, whose origins are associated with disturbance of the 'winds'[42], come from some a certain unfortunate event and are associated with the Wind God. The Wind God at one time was traveling around and he saw the princess Norbu Zinpba (which means in Tibetan 'Holder of the Jewels). She was also a goddess associated with the wind. The Wind God hadn't met her before and when looked upon her, she was incredibly beautiful, ornamented by different jewels, and there arose within him a desire towards Norbu Zinpba. They entered into a relationship; specifically they embraced in a sexual way. Just as they were having sex, he lost his grip on the 'Bladder of the Wind', which held in the forces of the wind, and of course, it opened up and they spilled out. This is the source all wind illnesses. This is why the source of wind illnesses is excessive desire.

The origin of the diseases associated with the bile is also associated with a certain king. He was a historical king. His name was Sherab Tengpo Sheten. Sheten means 'firm wisdom'. He decided to make a great offering ceremony to the gods and the great rishis (yogis). He invited them and they all arrived one by one. They came in front of the king to receive their offerings. It so happened that the god Shiva ended up

---

[42] 'Lung', in Tibetan.

178

at the end of the line. He was very unhappy with this and thought: "now I am the preeminent god of the world, and I shouldn't be at the end of the line." There arose within Shiva a great anger. Now, this was a very auspicious event that the king Sheten put together. There were beautiful, extensive offerings. The guests were also very auspicious; there were all of these wonderful gods, goddesses, and rishis. However, Shiva at the line was getting very angry, his eyes blazing forth with anger and, from the center of his forehead, he shot out a stream of fire. The fire burned up all the offerings and dispersed the crowd, incinerating them, or chasing them off, in any case the whole beautiful event was ruined by his anger. This is the origin of the rise in the bile element. We can understand from this, just as all those good things lost from Shiva's anger, the nature of anger, and the rise of bile. When the bile gets too great, anger arises. The bile is associated with the presence of strong anger.

The third category of illness is that of phlegm. This also has an origin. The introduction phlegm illnesses into the world are associated with a king of the ancient times. His name was Gyalway Ming. He had a beautiful queen whose name was Remaya. He also had a minister whose name was Tongo Chien. The queen and the minister struck up a friendship, which eventually came to the notice of King Gyalway Ming. The king became angry as he thought they were too friendly, so to speak. His anger resulted in having the queen and minister taken out into the middle of the ocean and tossed overboard. As this was occurring, Remaya and Tongo Chien said a prayer (monlam, which is a type of a prayer). They prayed that the king, who they referred to as 'nasty and insufferable', be beset with an incurable

179

illness of the nagas. The illnesses that are said to arise from the influence of the nagas or from any sort of local deities are then associated with the phlegm category. The force of their prayer, which was very strong and focused, produced the desired effect. The naga disease indeed struck the king. This was the first phlegm illness to enter the world. From that time on phlegm, illnesses have spread throughout the world. In the former accounts of the wind and the bile illnesses, it is clear how strong desire gave rise to the wind illnesses and strong anger gave rise to the bile illnesses. Here the present story illustrates how delusion (or ignorance) gives rise to the phlegm illnesses. It is not as clear here, and that is the nature of delusion. No parties, that is to say the king, queen, and minister, were clear as to an appropriate resolution of events. They could have been clearer in their thinking. This event is indicative of disturbances of the mind. Therefore, this event is associated with the generation of all phlegm illnesses.

Now, back on page six, the last line says: "May all sentient beings come to enjoy that great happiness and bliss which is complete freedom from illness. This is the goal: understanding the causes of illnesses, both general and specific, and because they have ultimate causes, the causes can be removed. Illnesses are not inherent. They are not inevitable. By removing the causes of illnesses, we can produce, ultimately, a state of happiness and bliss that is free from all illness.

We continue on page seven. It refers here to the meditation one does in conjunction with the recitation of the mantra. The first thing one does is the invocation of the Medicine Buddha together with his retinue, including all eight of the Medicine Buddhas and their retinues. They are invoked through the recitation of the mantras. The recitation of the mantra also serves as an exhortation, asking for their blessings. From doing this, innumerable rays of light come forth from the three places of their bodies (the crown of the head, the throat, and the heart). These rays of light purify sentient beings by the specific focus of one's concern in this practice, which is the welfare of living beings in the six realms of samsara without exception. Sentient beings function as one's chief object of concern. All sentient beings, from beginningless time, have accumulated various types of defilements and obscurations by virtue of karma and kleshas[43]. In addition to defilements and obscurations, there arise three different types of manifest problems. The three manifest problems are the illnesses, demons, and the degeneration of one's sacred commitments. The innumerable rays of light clear all of these away, which stream forth from the three places in the bodies of the Medicine Buddha and his retinue upon our request, which comes through our recitation of the mantra. Having thus purified all sentient beings in this way of the underlying and manifest unwholesome qualities, then the blessings of the Buddha and his retinue enter into them and establish the realization of samadhi. Samadhi is the meditative concentration and the full realization of all the qualities associated with the Medicine Buddha and his retinue. All of this is realized, or established within the mindstreams of oneself and other living beings through this recitation of the mantra.

---

[43] The activities that sentient beings engage in are their karma. Kleshas are unwholesome mental states such as greed, hatred, and ignorance.

Now, on pages eight and nine is the long form of the mantra recitation. Following that on page ten is the short mantra. Whichever of these one can do, then one does it as many times as possible at his point in the practice. Whether it is a few minutes or a few hours, you do as many as you can. As you do it, of course, you do the meditation as described understanding that the recitation of the mantra is the invoking of the blessings of the Medicine Buddhas and their retinues, exhorting them to send forth these rays of purifying light, removing the obscurations, diseases, demons, and so forth. This gives rise to the true realization of the meditation on the qualities of the Medicine Buddha. Therefore, thinking in those terms one does the recitation, then on page ten there's the conclusion of that meditation practice. At the conclusion, one visualizes each of the retinues of the Medicine Buddhas in turn dissolving into the Medicine Buddhas and they dissolve into the next one, and finally into the (main) Medicine Buddha himself. Then from the three places of the Medicine Buddha again come forth rays of light in the three colors (white at the crown, red at the throat, and blue at the heart). The nectar of pure awareness or the light of perfect wisdom then enters respectively into the three places of one's own body. Dissolving into one's three places, it gets rid of the three types of obstacles. It gets rid of the three obstacles. What are the three obstacles? They are the karmic obscurations arising from actions, from the unwholesome states of greed, anger, and delusion, which are the obscurations to omniscience. They are removed through the blessings of the rays of light. Once the obscurations are removed, the Medicine Buddha dissolves into light and the light enters into the

182

crown of one's head. With this, one's self becomes inseparable and undifferentiated from the Medicine Buddha himself. That is to say, that one becomes inseparable from the Buddha who is the embodiment of the omniscience and universal compassion of all enlightened beings, of all the Buddhas. Following that you rest your mind in 'Mahamudra'[44], which is the 'emptiness in form'. This is the defining quality of the realization of Mahamudra. That emptiness arises as form. In other words, one realizes that emptiness is not other than form. Through that understanding, one realizes the relative identity of form and emptiness. This is similar to what is written in the Heart Sutra where it says "Form is emptiness, emptiness is form..." only here it is just saying emptiness is form. If the form that we see is emptiness, then it follows very easily that form is emptiness. Therefore, in that state of realization one rests the mind at this point of focusing on the Great Seal, the Mahamudra, which is characterized by this realization. With everything dissolving into emptiness, you rest the mind in that nature of perfect awareness, the union of form and emptiness.

Upon the completion of that meditation, all that is left to do is the dedication. The dedication, first of all, is a dedication of the merit of this practice to one's own swift attainment of the state of the Medicine Buddha. Then, having attained that state, one resolves to establish all sentient beings, without exception, in that highest state of the Medicine Buddha.

---

[44] The literal translation of Mahamudra is 'Great Seal'.

Questions and Answers

Question: "Can you explain the difference between the long and short mantra?"

Answer: "It is always good to begin by saying the long one at least three times, or, if you have the opportunity, seven times or more. Then when you go for the actual accumulation of repetition of the mantra, you just do the short one."

Question: There seems to be an obvious qualitative difference between the long and short mantras, can you explain that difference?"

Answer: "There is not really a qualitative difference as it is a quantitative one. The meaning of both of them is the same, but the meaning is drawn out more explicitly in the long one."

Question: "What is the number of repetitions required to complete the practice of Medicine Buddha?"

Answer: (Rinpoche giggles here) "More than one!" (Now laughing out loud). "If one is not enough, then, do more!"

At this point, Ontul Rinpoche requested all attendees to begin the practice. "And now we try (laughing again)."

Further Reading

Here are few books as suggested reading. There are, of course, many other books on the subjects of these oral commentaries.

Vision and Transformation: An Introduction to the Buddha's Noble Eightfold Path by Sangharakshita. Windhorse Publications 1990

The Great Path Of Awakening by Jamgon Kongtrul Translated by Ken McLeod. Shambala Publications 1987. This book has in its appendix, the root text, which was translated by the Nalanda Translation Committee.

Training The Mind In The Great Way by Gyalwa Gendun Druppa the First Dalai Lama Translated by Glenn H. Mullin Snow Lion Publications 1993

A Guide To The Bodhisattva's Way Of Life, by Shantideva. Translated by Stephen Batchelor. Library of Tibetan Works & Archives Dharamsala 1979

Elaborations On Emptiness: Uses of the Heart Sutra Donald S. Lopez Jr. Editor Princeton University Press 1996

Transformation Of Suffering: A Handbook For Practitioners by Khenchen Könchog Gyaltshen Rinpoche Vajra Publications 1996